A Disciple-Making Christmas

General Editor: Brian Schulenburg

Copyright © 2016 Woodbury Community Church

Printed by CreateSpace.

ISBN: 1540440141
ISBN-13: 978-1540440143

All rights reserved. This book or any portion thereof may not be reproduced or used in any manner whatsoever without the express written permission of the editor except for the use of brief quotations in an article, book review, or report under International and Pan-American Copyright Conventions.

Unless otherwise indicated, all Scripture quotations are from the ESV® Bible (The Holy Bible, English Standard Version®), copyright © 2001 by Crossway, a publishing ministry of Good News Publishers. Used by permission. All rights reserved.

Scripture quotations marked (NASB) taken from the New American Standard Bible® (NASB), Copyright © 1960, 1962, 1963, 1968, 1971, 1972, 1973, 1975, 1977, 1995 by The Lockman Foundation, Used by permission. www.Lockman.org

Scripture quotations marked (NIV) are taken from the Holy Bible, New International Version®, NIV®. Copyright © 1973, 1978, 1984, 2011 by Biblica, Inc.™ Used by permission of Zondervan. All rights reserved worldwide. www.zondervan.com The "NIV" and "New International Version" are trademarks registered in the United States Patent and Trademark Office by Biblica, Inc.™

Scripture quotations marked (NKJV) are taken from the New King James Version®. Copyright © 1982 by Thomas Nelson. Used by permission. All rights reserved.

DEDICATION

This book is dedicated to the memory of Joan Hargis. Joan was a faithful member of Woodbury Community Church for many years. Her love for the Lord, her family, and her church family was evident to all who knew her. Joan had a special love in her heart for those who didn't yet know Christ. She wanted everyone to know the truth of the Gospel of Jesus Christ. She loved God's Word, the gift of prayer and the gift of poetry. She shared all three so generously. Joan will be missed this Christmas season.

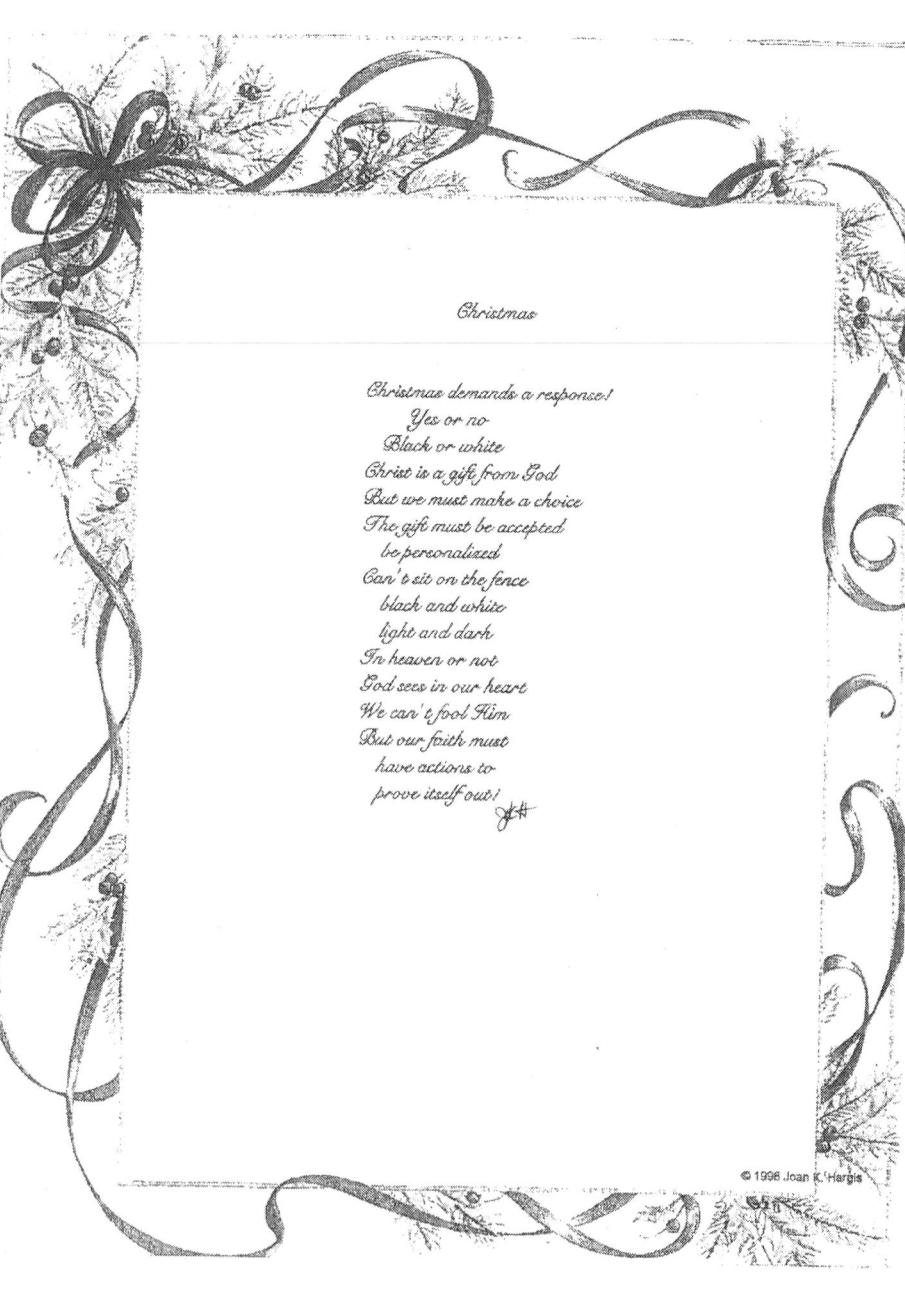

Christmas

Christmas demands a response!
   Yes or no
    Black or white
Christ is a gift from God
But we must make a choice
The gift must be accepted
   be personalized
Can't sit on the fence
   black and white
   light and dark
In heaven or not
God sees in our heart
We can't fool Him
But our faith must
   have actions to
   prove itself out!

© 1996 Joan K. Hergis

CONTENTS

	Acknowledgments	i
	Introduction	1
	Prologue – (The Saturday Before the First Day of Advent):"A Time of Preparation," Peter Akinboro	3
1	Day 1 (The First Sunday of Advent): "A Relationship Like No Other," Brian Schulenburg	5
2	Day 2: "The Joy of Giving," Pam Faessler	8
3	Day 3: "The Cost of Discipleship," Brian Schulenburg	12
4	Day 4: "Creating Space for God to Speak to You," Sara Lein	15
5	Day 5: "A Disciple-Making Marriage," Brian Schulenburg	18
6	Day 6: "The Priority of God's Word," Joe Dellaria	21
7	Day 7: "A Disciple-Making Family," Sally Mattison	25
8	Day 8 (The Second Sunday of Advent): "Experiencing 'Godly Possibilities' Through Prayer," Joan Haugen	29
9	Day 9: "Shining the Light at School," Marie McNamara	33
10	Day 10: "Feasting by Fasting," Grant Snyder	36
11	Day 11: "A Work-life That Honors God," Cyndi Schulenburg	39
12	Day 12: "The Gift of Healing," Alisa Rabin Bell	42
13	Day 13: "Impacting the World in Your Back Yard," Kari Bennet	46
14	Day 14: "The Gift of Sabbath," JJ Wessman	50
15	Day 15 (The Third Sunday of Advent): "Your Undeniable Mission Field," Holly Price	53

16	Day 16: "Be Still and Know – The Discipline of Silence," Darrin Geier	55
17	Day 17: "To Love an Enemy," Peter Akinboro	58
18	Day 18: "Choosing Less," Drew Mattison	61
19	Day 19: "Discipled Through Addiction (A Testimony)" Richard Minette	64
20	Day 20: "Confession is Good for the Soul," Melanie Snyder	69
21	Day 21: "God's Heart for the Widow," Stephanie Wesssman	72
22	Day 22 (The Fourth Sunday of Advent): "How Biblical Hospitality Could Change the World," Tammie Haveman	75
23	Day 23: "Spiritual Orphans," Jason Nygren	79
24	Day 24: "Self-Examination," Joe Dellaria	82
25	Day 25: "Loving Society's Throwaways," Grant Snyder	86
26	Day 26: "A Heart of Gratitude," Shane McNamara	90
27	Day 27: "God's Heart for the Oppressed," Joe Dellaria	93
28	Day 28: "The Discipline of Celebration," Liz Nelson	97
29	Day 29 (Christmas Day): "Divine Appointments," Brian Schulenburg	100

ACKNOWLEDGMENTS

There are many people whose work goes into the publishing of a book. This book is no exception. Thank you to Kelsey Holm, our editor extraordinaire, for reading through each of the Advent devotionals and making the necessary changes. Thank you to Radleigh Wakefield, our graphic designer who created the cover art. Thank you to Bill Hargis for donating some of Joan's poems for inclusion in this book.

Thank you to Peter Akinboro, Alisa Rabin Bell, Kari Bennett, Joe Dellaria, Pam Faessler, Darrin Geier, Joan Haugen, Tammie Haveman, Sara Lein, Shane and Marie McNamara, Drew and Sally Mattison, Richard Minette, Liz Nelson, Jason Nygren, Holly Price, Cyndi Schulenburg, Grant and Melanie Snyder, and JJ and Stephanie Wessman, our contributing authors. Your devotionals are inspiring. What a talented group of writers you are! Each of you are making an impact in this generation. I am blessed to have the opportunity to pastor such an extraordinary group of individuals.

Thank you most of all to Jesus Christ, our Savior, whose birth we celebrate this Christmas season. It is because of you that we have hope. You are our source of strength, our joy, and our delight.

- Pastor Brian Schulenburg

A DISCIPLE-MAKING CHRISTMAS

INTRODUCTION

When I was a young youth pastor serving at a church in Illinois, the senior pastor encouraged our congregation to take a 40-day spiritual adventure. Individuals and families spent 40 days reading through the same material, praying similar prayers and hearing the same sermon each Sunday. At the end of the 40 days, our congregation had grown deeper in our faith, closer in our relationships and more focused on our mission.

A while back, God began to place a burden on my heart for a similar thing to happen at the church that I pastor in Minnesota. As I began to think about when a good time would be for our church to take a spiritual adventure, the Advent season stuck in my brain.

Christmas has been called the most wonderful time of the year. In most churches, this is a season of joyous expectation. We spend the four Sundays prior to Christmas Eve focusing on the themes of expectation, hope, joy and love. This tradition dates back to the Protestant reformer Martin Luther. As a child, I would look forward to Christmas Day by opening the flaps of the Advent calendar that my mom purchased for us each year. Each day a new surprise, typically a small piece of chocolate, would be revealed, as the days leading toward Christmas came to an end.

The purpose of this devotional book is to help us focus on Jesus' Great Commission to make disciples. We define a disciple as someone who loves God, loves people and joins Jesus in his mission of making more disciples. We'll spend the Advent season looking at the relationships that God has strategically placed in our lives, and the opportunities that we have to grow in our personal walk with Him. Each day we will focus on a specific relationship that God has called us to think about in terms of His mission, or a spiritual habit that will help us grow deeper in our love for Him. Not every relationship will apply directly to you. On a day that focuses on a relationship that doesn't apply to your life, pray for those who do have those relationships.

Each day, as you are reading these devotions, written by different people from the church that I serve, think of them as a little surprise—a gift for you each day. God's Word is sweeter than honey (Psalm 17:7-11; 119:103). May you delight in these meditations from God's Word as much as I delighted in finding that little piece of chocolate in the Advent calendar so many years ago.

Enjoy . . . "A Disciple-Making Christmas!"

Brian Schulenburg
Senior Pastor
Woodbury Community Church
Woodbury, Minn.

PROLOGUE: A TIME OF PREPARATION

THE SATURDAY BEFORE THE FIRST DAY OF ADVENT— PETER AKINBORO

Each time my family watches "The Passion of the Christ," I witness similar reactions. There is usually a quick, quiet moment of self-assessment—and no matter how well-behaved you think you've been, you'll always feel you fall short of the grace we received through his suffering. Hence, the following outburst of emotions and prayers, for forgiveness and help to live a life worthy of the suffering of our Savior. The movie is a reminder of Christ's sacrifice for us, but a better reminder is the celebration of his birth. At Christmas, we should remember that he was born for the sole purpose of dying to give us life.

When people fall sick, they usually do a mental retrace of what made them sick or what they did wrong. We want to know if it was something we ate or some stress we put our body through. This self-diagnosis is not always correct, but it sometimes helps us avoid repeating anything that jeopardizes our health. In the same vein, the word of God enjoins us to do a regular spiritual examination of ourselves, to avoid spiritual ill-health that can adversely affect us.

God asked Joshua to examine the nation of Israel when Achan violated God's command and got the nation into trouble (Joshua 6: 18-7:14). "… There is an accursed thing in your midst, O Israel; you cannot stand before your enemies until you take away the accursed thing from among you. In the morning therefore you shall be brought according to your tribes. And it shall be that the tribe which the Lord takes shall come by households; and the household which the Lord takes shall come man by man … " (NKJV). The Israelites examined themselves—but only after disaster had struck. However, as a result, they overcame their enemies.

God's message to the seven churches in Revelation 2-3 are calls for self-examination, drawing their attention to areas where they are weak and lagging, and warning them. "How can a young man cleanse his way? By taking heed according to Your word" (Psalm 119:9). We need to daily assess our actions and motives by the word of God. Christmastime is the season to recall the course of the ending year and the prospects of the approaching new year, to examine and rededicate our lives.

FAMILY DISCUSSION

- How can remembering Christ's death in the season of celebrating Christ's birth help us appreciate this time of year even more?
- What are some areas in your life where you know you need God's help to live better?
- Make a decision to regularly ask God for help in these areas.

PRAYER

Dear Lord,

Search us and know our hearts! Try us and know our thoughts! See if there be any grievous way in us, and lead us in the way everlasting!

In Jesus' name, Amen.

A RELATIONSHIP LIKE NO OTHER

THE FIRST DAY OF ADVENT—BRIAN SCHULENBURG

And the angel said to her, "Do not be afraid, Mary, for you have found favor with God. 31 And behold, you will conceive in your womb and bear a son, and you shall call his name Jesus. 32 He will be great and will be called the Son of the Most High. And the Lord God will give to him the throne of his father David, 33 and he will reign over the house of Jacob forever, and of his kingdom there will be no end" (Luke 1:30-33).

I've always wondered whether or not there was a conversation. Did God the Father and God the Son talk about the Father's plan to redeem mankind? Did God the Holy Spirit participate in the conversation, contributing to the unique role that He too would play in God's redemptive story?

I can picture the opening . . . "Jesus, my one and only Son, I have a plan . . ."

There has never been a relationship, nor will there ever be a relationship, quite like the relationship between the three members of our Triune God. Christians throughout the centuries have believed that God has eternally existed in three persons—Father, Son and Holy Spirit. God didn't create Adam because He needed help (Acts 17:24-25). He didn't create Adam because He was incomplete in any way. He didn't create Adam because He was lonely (Genesis 1:26). He didn't create Adam because He was unfulfilled. So, why? Why did God create Adam, knowing that Adam would sin and that Adam's sin would bring separation from God (Romans 5:12)?

That's a good question. Even King David wondered about that. In Psalm 8:3-4, David wrote, "When I look at your heavens, the work of your fingers, the moon and the stars, which you have set in place, what is man that you are mindful of him, and the son of man that you care for him?"

God created Adam for His glory and because of His great love. Did you know that Jeremiah 31:3 says that God has loved us with an everlasting love? Before you were born, God knew you and loved you (Psalm 139:13-18).

Christmas is the story of God the Son becoming a man. John 1:14 says, "And the Word became flesh and dwelt among us, and we have seen his glory, glory as of the only Son from the Father, full of grace and truth."

The perfect relationship that exists between God the Father, God the Son and God the Holy Spirit is something that Jesus wants us to experience too. Even though our lives have been scarred by the effects of sin, we can be made right with God. We can be seen as perfect before Him because of the gift of salvation that Jesus offers through His death, burial and resurrection. The Son came full of grace and truth. This Advent season we will focus on God's grace and His truth. We'll examine what it means to make disciples in the various relationships in our lives. We'll look at how to grow in our love for Jesus.

FAMILY DISCUSSION

- What do you think the relationship between God the Father, God the Son and God the Holy Spirit looks like?
- What would it look like for you to commit the next 30 days of your life to intentionally live for God's glory?
- How does the Christmas season demonstrate God's love to you?

PRAYER

Dear Heavenly Father,

Thank you for the gift of Jesus. Thank you for your plan to deal with my sin through sending your Son, Jesus, to earth to die for my sins. Help me live my life for your glory. This Christmas season, help me grow in my love for you, my love for others and my desire to join you in your mission of making more disciples for Jesus Christ.

In Jesus' name, Amen.

THE JOY OF GIVING

THE SECOND DAY OF ADVENT—PAM FAESSLER

11 And going into the house, they saw the child with Mary his mother, and they fell down and worshiped him. Then, opening their treasures, they offered him gifts, gold and frankincense and myrrh (Matthew 2:11).

I have a small nativity set that sits on the toy shelf all year 'round for my grandchildren to play with. They love to talk about Mary and Jesus and, like all small children, they treasure the sheep and their shepherd. They pretend that the Wise Men take a long journey from the shelf, over the carpet and to the table where everyone is waiting for them to arrive and bring their gifts. What small child wouldn't find that part of the story exciting?

But that isn't the purpose of the Magi being included in the Christmas story.

I picture the Magi dressed in elaborate clothes, with hats or crowns on their heads, and scarves wrapped around their necks, protecting them from the elements. They walk alongside camels carrying packs filled with supplies for their long journey from the Far East, heading toward

Jerusalem, the city where they imagined the King of the Jews to reign. This visual picture comes from the many nativities and illustrations I have seen portraying these famous men. The Bible doesn't tell us how many Magi there were or give us their names or tell us what cities they lived in, but it does tell us that they responded to God's sign, a star placed in the sky, directing them to their destination, the home of Mary and Joseph.

Do you ever wonder if others saw the star but did not respond?

These men weren't Israelites, but intellectuals from the East who the bible tells us knew the stories of the coming of the King of the Jews. They followed the star in the hope of meeting royalty and with the desire to worship Him.

The Magi were certainly not who the Israelites would have expected to be invited to meet their Messiah and be an important part the story we celebrate in churches every year! We sing songs about these famous men!

When they arrived in Jerusalem, they learned that the child was not there, but in Bethlehem, the place from which the prophet, Micah, had said the ruler of Israel would come. How much they actually realized at the time is not known, but we do know that they believed enough to protect the Christ child from the jealous King Herod and his evil plan to rid the world of a threat to his kingdom.

Sometimes God allows detours so we can be certain of where He is really taking us.

They left Jerusalem and the star once again appeared to guide them until it came to rest over the home of the young child. In the book of Matthew we are told that when they saw the star they were overjoyed. Can you imagine their excitement as the long journey finally came to an end and they were in the place where they would meet the ruler of a nation?

When they saw the child, Jesus, with His mother, Mary, they fell down and worshipped the King, realizing this precious babe was worthy of their praise. They were meeting the Christ, the Messiah who was sent by God to restore His relationship with man.

This testimony reminds me that whenever I encounter Jesus, I need to be in awe of His joyful presence!

Then the Magi presented their treasures, gifts that they felt would be worthy of giving to the King—gold, frankincense and myrrh. They did not bring clothing or something for the child to play with. They brought extravagant things that could perhaps provide for His future needs.

The Bible tells us that after this, they traveled home, taking a different route to avoid another encounter with King Herod. We don't know how long they stayed in Bethlehem. We don't know anything else about these men.

I like to think that the Magi told their story to everyone they met on their long journey home, how they had traveled to meet the child who is the King and that they worshipped Him and experienced His joy, that they were preparing the way for others to recognize God's light, which reveals the journey He has planned for their lives.

What joy!

Now, when my grandchildren get the nativity out, I hope they want to act out the excitement of seeing God's light directing them to Jesus. I hope they'll realize that only the King is worthy of praise and that they would see Jesus as the true gift giver that will fill their lives with uncontainable joy!

FAMILY DISCUSSION

- Where is God calling you to go?
- Do you follow Jesus with an attitude of joy?
- With whom can you share God's gift of joy?

PRAYER

Thank you Lord, that you call all men to follow you. Like the Magi, call us out and send us to the places where you are. May our hearts' desire be to worship only you, Jesus, and that we would be humbled in your presence. May you be the treasure that we give to others, with the joy of knowing that if they accept your gift of good news you will change the direction of their lives forever.

Amen

THE COST OF DISCIPLESHIP

THE THIRD DAY OF ADVENT—BRIAN SCHULENBURG

20 I have been crucified with Christ. It is no longer I who live, but Christ who lives in me. And the life I now live in the flesh I live by faith in the Son of God, who loved me and gave himself for me (Galatians 2:20).

One of my favorite things to do at Christmastime is to visit the homes of my friends. I love seeing the different ways people decorate for Christmas. Like most people, I suppose my favorite decoration is the Christmas tree. Why? Because each tree is so different. It doesn't matter how many homes I go into, the primary Christmas tree in each home is thoroughly unique. Some trees are decorated with simple white lights and beautiful glass ornaments. Other trees are a menagerie of colorful lights and homemade ornaments. When our kids were growing up, we gave each one of them a Christmas ornament each year. The ornament usually had something to do with an activity that our kids were involved with over the course of the past 12 months. Our tree was a glorious collection of mismatched ornaments that meant very little to anyone outside of our family, but meant the world to us.

On our tree is one ornament that seems a bit misplaced during the Christmas season. It is a replica of the stake that a Roman executioner would have used during a crucifixion. The ornament is large, but somewhat understated. I don't think we have ever had a guest comment on that particular ornament. The Hallmark Keepsakes with Frank Sinatra singing, Darth Vader holding his light saber or the beeps of the Galaga video game ornament garner lots of attention. The simple stake? Nothing.

But that stake is a reminder to me of what Christmas is all about. Jesus was born in the shadow of a cross. He was born to die. Just as Christ was called to die on a cross for our sin, so we, as disciples of Jesus, have been called to a crucifixion. In Galatians 2:20, the Apostle Paul told a local church that he had been crucified with Christ. His life was no longer his own. He was living, by faith, for Christ. Paul knew that Jesus loved and gave himself for him.

In Luke 9:23-25 we read of Jesus, "And he said to all, 'If anyone would come after me, let him deny himself and take up his cross daily and follow me. For whoever would save his life will lose it, but whoever loses his life for my sake will save it. For what does it profit a man if he gains the whole world and loses or forfeits himself?'"

Jesus loved and gave Himself for you. Will you live for Him?

Maybe getting a stake, putting a ribbon on it, and tying it up on your Christmas tree will remind you of the sacrifice that Jesus paid for you—and the sacrifice He is asking you to make for Him.

FAMILY DISCUSSION

- What do you think the Apostle Paul meant when he said that he had been crucified with Christ?
- Why do you think Jesus told the disciples to take up their crosses daily? What would that mean in your life?
- Would your priorities look different if you were living the type of life that Jesus and Paul talk about in Luke 9:23-25 and Galatians 2:20?

PRAYER

Dear Heavenly Father,

Sometimes it's hard to remember at Christmastime that Jesus was born in the shadow of a cross. Help me remember that being a follower of Christ means that I too have been born in the shadow of a cross. Help me to courageously live my life in such a way that you would receive glory and honor and that your name would be lifted up as I take up my cross to follow you.

In Jesus' name, Amen.

CREATING SPACE FOR GOD TO SPEAK TO YOU

THE FOURTH DAY OF ADVENT—SARA LEIN

And rising very early in the morning, while it was still dark, he departed and went out to a desolate place, and there he prayed (Mark 1:35).

'Tis the season for holiday decorating, baking, gift buying-wrapping-giving, family gatherings, holiday parties, Christmas cards and so much more! These are joy-bringing, mood-setting activities and events that have been created with good intentions to help us celebrate Christmas. However, in the midst of this hectic holiday pace, how do we keep our hearts and minds set on the true meaning of the season?

Somewhere along the way, we need to create a space for stillness—for listening—for seeking the will of God.

"Suddenly a great company of the heavenly host appeared with the angel, praising God and saying, 'Glory to God in the highest heaven, and on earth peace to those on whom his favor rests.' When the angels had left them and gone into heaven, the shepherds said to one another,

'Let's go to Bethlehem and see this thing that has happened, which the Lord has told us about.' So they hurried off and found Mary and Joseph, and the baby, who was lying in the manger. When they had seen him, they spread the word concerning what had been told them about this child, and all who heard it were amazed at what the shepherds said to them. But Mary treasured up all these things and pondered them in her heart. The shepherds returned, glorifying and praising God for all the things they had heard and seen, which were just as they had been told" (Luke 2:13-20 - NIV).

The angels were praising, the shepherds were glorifying—and Mary treasured up these things and pondered them in her heart. In awe of the greatness of this holy child, she paused, she reflected, she honored the gift from God. We need to reflect as Mary did, treasuring this gift of Jesus, our Savior, pondering His greatness and the impact on our lives.

Years later, Jesus, the Savior of the world, busy with the activities of His life—teaching, healing, serving, creating miracles, saving sinners—paused to connect with his father. "And rising very early in the morning, while it was still dark, he departed and went out to a desolate place, and there he prayed" (Mark 1:35).

Why pause? Why pray? Why create space for stillness? This is when we hear God speak. Jesus knew the importance of communicating with His father. He drew away into a quiet space to pray. He sought the wisdom and comfort gained through those intimate moments together.

Just as Jesus longed to converse with His father, God, Our Father," longs to communicate with us. As our Creator, our Savior, He has a plan for each one of us. Spending time in quiet reflection provides the opportunity for Him to speak truth into our lives.

During this holiday season, as we frantically seek to make this the best Christmas yet, let us put the festive to-do list down for a bit. Instead, let us spend time with Jesus. We should treasure and ponder as Mary did. We need to be open to the messages He has for us—to intentionally seek His will and listen closely for His instructions. Let's ask for direction in our lives—and wait for His response. We ought to linger in the love, care and acceptance He has for us.

Let's light some candles and sit in the peace of a holy night, in conversation with our Savior.

FAMILY DISCUSSION

- What do you think Mary was thinking, as she treasured all that was happening as she became the mother of the Savior of the world?
- Why was it so important for Jesus to go away to a quiet place to pray to his father?
- How can we create space in our busy lives to hear God speak to us?

PRAYER

Dear Lord,

Thank you so much for loving us. Forgive us for leading lives that are often so busy, we forget to create space for you. We desire to know you and to hear your voice. We commit to communicating with you throughout our days and to being still and silent enough to receive your word. We seek your truth. Help us know your will and feel your peace.

Amen.

A DISCIPLE-MAKING MARRIAGE

THE FIFTH DAY OF ADVENT—BRIAN SCHULENBURG

31 "Therefore a man shall leave his father and mother and hold fast to his wife, and the two shall become one flesh" (Ephesians 5:31).

There is an old prayer with which I close almost every wedding ceremony. In that prayer is a line that reads, "Teach this couple that marriage is not merely for each other; it is two joining hands to serve you. Give them a great spiritual purpose in life. May they seek first your Kingdom and your righteousness, and trust that as they do, you will take care of the rest."

The marriage relationship should be the most beautiful relationship that we will experience on planet earth. It is also the most challenging. Marriage is a gift, instituted by God—a picture of the relationship that God has with his bride, the church.

When Cyndi and I first got married, I had no idea what God would bring our way. No couple does. Over the past 25 years we have had our share of joy and heartache, of celebration and weeping. Through it all, we have grown so much. In my life, Cyndi is the person who knows me better than anyone else. She is also the person who has impacted my walk with Jesus more than anyone else.

All marriages have the potential to experience that. This Christmas season, as we focus on the many relationships that God has placed in our lives, may you who are married commit anew to praying for your spouse. Pray that they might become more like Jesus. As you pray for your spouse, pray that you might also become more like Christ. If God has blessed you with children, pray that they would become a little bit more like Jesus this Christmas season.

Of all the things that Cyndi and I have done as a couple, there are a few that bring me the most joy. I rejoice that all four of our kids know Jesus. A disciple-making marriage is one where a husband and wife join hands in praying for the spiritual nurture of their children. Jesus is talked about in the home, and modeled in our lives.

I also rejoice in shared mission. I am grateful that Cyndi has a heart for our kids' friends. Some of our greatest days as a family have been the ones in which we've had the opportunity to share Christ's love with our children's friends. A disciple-making marriage can impact dozens of homes with the truth of the gospel. Find ways this season to incorporate friends who need Jesus into your Christmas celebration. As a family, pray that God might give you the opportunity to share together in a great spiritual mission.

FAMILY DISCUSSION

- If you are married, how has your marriage helped you grow in your relationship with Jesus Christ?
- How do you think marriage is a picture of the love that Christ has for his church?
- What is your family's mission? Do you have a great spiritual purpose in life? If not, take a few minutes to pray about what that could be.

PRAYER

Dear Heavenly Father,

Thank you for the gift of marriage. Thank you that, in marriage, two join together as one. May our family be a family that brings joy to you. May you help us live every day of this Advent season in the awareness of and obedience to your mission for us.

In Jesus' Name, Amen.

THE PRIORITY OF GOD'S WORD

THE SIXTH DAY OF ADVENT—JOE DELLARIA

105 Your word is a lamp to my feet and a light to my path (Psalm 119:105).

A few years ago, I received a five-pack of small LED flashlights for Christmas. At first, I thought it was a pretty cool gift until I tried to use them. It turned out the best way to turn them on was to put the batteries in and drop them. That always worked. The on-off switch was there just to taunt the user. Even if you got it to turn on, the light would randomly stop and start. The flashlights were virtually useless. Eventually they all found their way to the trash bin. I went out and spent about three times the amount on one good LED flashlight. It turns on and off when you hit the switch and shines brightly until I turn it off. I mounted this on my drill press so I can clearly see where and what I am drilling.

When I read today's passage, the first thing that popped into my mind is that God's Word, the Bible, is a flashlight that helps me see so I can do what God calls me to do. Obviously, I wasn't thinking about the five-pack set, but the more expensive one I bought later—the one that actually worked. While it is OK to take this insight from the passage, there's a deeper and more profound meaning here that shouldn't be missed.

As Pastor Brian consistently points out, context is king. That is, a passage is understood most accurately when looked at in the context of the passages before and after it. This is so true of this passage. So let's look at the verses leading up to Psalm 119:105.

"Oh how I love your law! It is my meditation all the day. Your commandment makes me wiser than my enemies, for it is ever with me. I have more understanding than all my teachers, for your testimonies are my meditation. I understand more than the aged, for I keep your precepts. I hold back my feet from every evil way, in order to keep your word. I do not turn aside from your rules, for you have taught me. How sweet are your words to my taste, sweeter than honey to my mouth! Through your precepts I get understanding; therefore I hate every false way.

"Your word is a lamp to my feet and a light to my path" (Psalm 119:97-105).

First, it is important to note that Verse 105 starts a new paragraph. This separates it from Verses 97-104, which reveal what the psalmist did before Verse 105. Here is a partial look at the psalmist's view of these Scriptures.

> Verse 97: He loves God's word and meditates on it "all the day."
> Verse 98: He is wiser because God's Word "is ever with me."
> Verse 99: He has more understanding because God's words "are my meditation."
> Verse 100: He has greater understanding than those who are older because "I keep your precepts." (He obeys God's commands.)
> Verse 101: Obeying God's Word keeps him from evil.
> Verse 102: He chooses to obey God's words, for they teach him.

Verse 103: God's word is "sweet"—that is, attractive and appealing.
- Verse 104: Understanding is gained through study, which leads him to hate evil.

These verses tell us what must happen to gain the benefit of Verse 105. What struck me is that Verses 97-104 show the great effort the psalmist took to know and follow God's Word. It became a lamp to his feet and a light to his path after doing that.

These verses tell us that if you desire for God to lead you with his light, you must cherish, study, meditate, obey and apply his word. Only then does it become a light that provides wisdom and holiness. Those unwilling to pursue God's truths in that manner end up with a light like those in my five-pack LEDs. It works intermittently and does not light consistently.

As always, this is not about trying harder. This is about cherishing, valuing and yielding to God's Word to the point that you seek to know and understand it all day, every day—just as the psalmist did. Those who do this will be guided into all truth by the Holy Spirit (John 16:13).

FAMILY DISCUSSION

- What kind of "spiritual flashlight" do you have? Is yours more like my five-pack LEDs or the single, more expensive and affective light?
- Using the summaries of Verses 97-104, think about how you are preparing your "spiritual light."
- Share one thing you can do to raise the priority of the Bible in your life. How willing are you to commit to doing this? Are you willing to let someone hold you accountable to that?

PRAYER

Dear Heavenly Father,

Your Word is an incredible source of truth, wisdom, power and peace. I desire to receive all that you provide in your Word to transform my thinking and the way I live. I come before you and yield to you. I ask you to work in my heart to give me a love for you and your word that will draw me to read, study, believe and apply your word. I ask that the Holy Spirit will give me strength and perseverance to read the Bible on a daily basis and lead me into all truth as I seek to do this. As I read your word, in the words of Psalm 43:3, I call on you to . . .

> "Send out your light and your truth;
> let them lead me;
> let them bring me to your holy hill
> and to your dwelling!"

In Jesus' name, Amen.

A DISCIPLE-MAKING FAMILY

THE SEVENTH DAY OF ADVENT—SALLY MATTISON

4 Tell to the coming generation the glorious deeds of the Lord, and his might, and the wonders that he has done (Psalm 78:4).

Jesus says, "Let the little children come to me, and do not hinder them, for the kingdom of God belongs to such as these. Truly I tell you, anyone who will not receive the kingdom of God like a little child will never enter it" (Mark 10:14-15 - NIV).

Last year, our once-shy daughter requested a major role in the Christmas program. She fell in love with the character, and with faith "like a little child," she trusted that God would help her do what she needed to portray this character that she loved. As the day approached, she boldly invited everyone she knew to the program—even the crossing guard at school. Frankly, I was a bit on pins and needles, but it was a huge encouragement to us as a family to see how God carried her through.

So often, whether we are involved with children as their mentors, friends, parents, aunts and uncles or grandparents, we tend to focus on the edict to "train a child in the way he should go" (Proverbs 22:6). For some, this becomes a prescription to have a certain amount of Bible study, prayer time and devotional time in the family. I, for one, have spent plenty of time disappointed in myself for not staying consistent in maintaining a family devotional time or not being diligent in teaching my children to effectively pray for others. As with all other realms of parenting and work with children, though, we all know there is no one instruction manual, no perfect handbook, no perfect formula. So it is with spiritual discipleship.

"To train" in the original Hebrew means to dedicate, and commentators argue that within the context of Proverbs, this speaks much more to a sustained and intentional shepherding of our children's hearts. I would argue there's also an implication of something unique in "the way he should go." We need to recognize that our guidance must be unique for each child. Even in studying God's Word, some children will more deeply apply God's Word if they read the Bible as a family, while others might better understand through messages, music or recorded Scripture. Moreover, enough cannot be said for the "teachable moments" in our lives—taking time to deeply answer the questions children ask and direct them back to Scripture for their answers, calling attention to the distinctions between society's priorities and biblical standards, or pointing them to Scripture when they are struggling with attitudes or behavior. While we pray as a family and typically read a Bible story and application before bed, I would guess my kids may have been more impacted by the number of times we've looked together at their "why" questions through a spiritual lens.

Ultimately, when we think of the "childlike faith" referenced in Mark—to "receive the kingdom of God like a little child"—we know faith is about truly trusting God and giving him control over your life. As guides for the children in our life, we need to find ways to connect their growing understanding of God's Word and His truth to an authentic faith lived life-on-life with others. We need to keep pointing them back to Scripture as the truth in their lives. At the same time, we need to recognize that God has also given us a gift through them—an opportunity to see how powerful a childlike faith can be. My daughter has taught me much about boldness. She is fearless in sharing her faith. In a public school, she has seized opportunities to perform Christian poetry, read multiple verses from Scripture and imbue much of her classwork with evidence of her faith. Leaning on her example, I have been bolder in sharing my faith, as when asked to share about identity in my graduate work at a public university. There, "Christian" seems like a bad word, even though the university's ideals align with biblical dictates of justice and defending the oppressed. Likewise, I have a strong sense that my son might help us grow in discernment. Though young and only a couple of years into his commitment to Christ, he is already asking questions about why we say "In God We Trust" when, as he says, "so many trust in the American dream."

While we as adults have much to share from our experience—"the glorious deeds of the Lord, and his might, and the wonders that he has done"—we also must always remember that we can learn from the children in our lives as well. Even little children can be a means for God's ability to use one another as "iron sharpens iron" (Proverbs 27:17). Together, we can all serve as a "disciple-making family."

FAMILY DISCUSSION

- What are some of the "glorious deeds" God has done in your life or the lives of the children you influence? How can you share those stories during this Christmas season?
- How have you seen God work in the children in your life? If their faith has encouraged you, have you shared that encouragement with them?
- What are some of the unique ways that God speaks to the children in your life? How can you uniquely guide them in their Bible study, application and life filled with faith?

PRAYER

Lord God,

Sometimes we get so caught up in the hustle and bustle that we forget to be intentional in our interactions with the children around us. This Christmas season, help us to not get so caught up in the festivities and gift-giving that we neglect to keep pointing our kids back to Christ—not just the miracle of His birth, but ultimately that He came to give us true life. Throughout the year, use our conversations to remind children of what God has done in their lives and our own, and the many ways He fuels us with wisdom, comfort, patience and joy.

In Jesus' name, Amen.

EXPERIENCING GODLY POSSIBILITIES THROUGH PRAYER

THE EIGHTH DAY OF ADVENT—JOAN HAUGEN

6 Do not be anxious about anything, but in everything, by prayer and petition, with thanksgiving, present your requests to God. 7 And the peace of God, which transcends all understanding, will guard your hearts and minds in Christ Jesus (Philippians 4:6-7 - NIV).

When my sister and I were in grade school and Christmastime rolled around, we could hardly wait to open our presents on Christmas morning, as was our family tradition. One year, when we were particularly impatient—and greedy—we found opportunity in a family friend's unexpected Christmas Eve visit. After asking, then begging, our mother to let us open "just one present" while our friend was there, we succeeded in gaining our mother's permission to open one gift. Upon opening it, we quickly asked if we could open another, to which our mother, worn down with Christmas fatigue, acquiesced. Encouraged by her answer, we continued in this fashion until nearly all our Christmas presents were open. Barely any remained under the tree to be opened the next morning.

Oh, my! What had we done?

What we had done was unlock the floodgate of gifts our mother had planned for, purchased, wrapped and set under the tree to give us on Christmas morning.

In a loving and genuine effort to create special Christmas experiences for her family and friends—and a desperate attempt to keep her sanity—our mother gave in to the selfish pestering of her greedy children. She intended to give us our gifts on Christmas morning, but she gave them to us on Christmas Eve because we begged for them. Right or wrong, she gave them to us because we asked.

In Matthew 7:7-11, Jesus teaches us that it is right to ask our Heavenly Father for gifts. "Ask and it will be given to you; seek and you will find; knock and the door will be opened to you. For everyone who asks receives; the one who seeks finds; and to the one who knocks, the door will be opened. 'Which of you, if your son asks for bread, will give him a stone? Or if he asks for a fish, will give him a snake? If you, then, though you are evil, know how to give good gifts to your children, how much more will your Father in heaven give good gifts to those who ask him!'" (NIV)

My mother is wonderful. And I'm sure the gifts she gave me and my sister that year were wonderful, too. But how much greater are the gifts from our precious heavenly Father! Ephesians 3:14-21 tells us that our wise, loving and gracious heavenly Father, out of His glorious riches, gives us immeasurably more than all we could ever ask or imagine. Things like the Holy Spirit, strength and power, Christ's dwelling in us, faith, love and the fullness of God. Those are amazing gifts!

I believe one of the greatest gifts our Father God makes available to us is the privilege of participating with Him in His divine nature. God has given us everything we need for life and godliness through our knowledge of him (2 Peter 1:3-4) and we can access all of these godly possibilities through prayer. Like this quote says, "When man PLANS, MAN works; When man PRAYS, GOD works." Whether we sincerely seek him in quiet, focused and intimate conversation, or as we're driving down the highway, by readily turning to God in prayer, we can play an active part in the things he wants to accomplish in our own hearts and lives—and in the hearts and lives of those for whom we pray.

As you grow in your faith, knowing God in ever increasing ways through Scripture reading and study, your prayers will grow, too. You will be more aware of God's amazing attributes, His ways, plans and promises. Your prayer life will also grow if you take time to study prayer, its purposes and strategies, and actually practice praying on your own and with others. You will begin to pray with more adoration, forgiveness, wisdom, boldness, expectancy and gratefulness. This genuine and active prayer life will allow you to see and take hold of the godly possibilities that are meant to be part of your life in Christ.

And don't forget! As you bring every big and little thing to God in prayer, he promises to guard your heart and mind with His peace, which transcends all understanding.

That's the kind of peace I think we'd all like to experience this Christmas!

FAMILY DISCUSSION

- What is one thing you could do to strengthen your prayer life?
- Is there a special issue, need or person in your life right now that you haven't taken to God in prayer? What might you ask God for as you pray about it?
- In what ways have you seen God answer your prayers? Is it what you expected?

PRAYER

Dear Heavenly Father,

Thank you that you love us and want us to come to you in prayer. Thank you that you always answer us with what is best and allow us to participate in your divine plans. Please help me come to you with all my joys and concerns, Lord, and guard my heart and mind with your perfect peace this Christmas and in the New Year.

In Jesus Name, Amen.

SHINING THE LIGHT AT SCHOOL

THE NINTH DAY OF ADVENT—MARIE MCNAMARA

12 When Jesus spoke again to the people, he said, "I am the light of the world. Whoever follows me will never walk in darkness, but will have the light of life" (John 8:12 - NIV).

Jesus tells us we will have the light of life if we follow Him. Sounds simple right? We follow Him and automatically we have the light. Sometimes that basic truth is difficult to practice. For a few weeks in seventh grade, my social studies class set up a mock congress where each student role-played as a senator. As senators, we wrote and voted on bills. And these bills often involved highly controversial topics. At the end of the project we voted on a bill written by the teacher, who played the role of president. The bill was written to legalize same-sex marriage. Keep in mind this was in 2003, so 12 years before same-sex marriage was actually legalized in all 50 states. Our charismatic teacher gave a very compelling argument for why same-sex marriage should be legalized. So when it came time to vote, he asked, "All in favor?" and almost every hand in the class went up. Then he asked "All opposed?"

and there was my lone hand raised in defiance to something I knew to be wrong.

Of course, at 12 years old, I had a hard time articulating to my friends why I thought it was wrong. All I knew was that I had been taught that marriage was between one man and one woman. Over the years I have done more studying and since learned it is a biblical truth laid out for us in Genesis 2 and reiterated in Matthew 19:5 when Jesus tells us that "For this reason a man will leave his father and mother and be united to his wife, and the two will become one flesh." (NIV)

It is important as students to know the truths of God, even when we can't back up our convictions like a professor of theology. No, we don't need to have all the answers. We just need to know what the Lord teaches. And it's just as important to stand up for what is right, especially when we are standing alone.

Parents, this puts a good deal of responsibility on you as well. Like I mentioned I only knew same-sex marriage was wrong because my parents talked with me about it. As parents, it is our duty to share the light and knowledge of Christ with our children. No child is expected to know the difference between right and wrong without being taught. And no one can be expected to stand up for what is right if they don't know right from wrong.

So today, as you think about what is right, and if it gets tough to do the right thing, remember Jesus' sobering words when he says, "If anyone is ashamed of me and my words in this adulterous and sinful generation, the Son of Man will be ashamed of them when he comes in his Father's glory with the holy angels" (Mark 8:38 - NIV).

FAMILY DISCUSSION

- How can you shine the light of Christ at school (or work) today?
- What is God telling you to stand up for?
- What is holding you back from standing up for what is right?

PRAYER

Lord,

Please give me the courage and strength to stand up for you today. Allow me to display your love in my school or workplace. Thank you for always being with me and standing by me, so I know I'm never alone.

Amen.

FEASTING BY FASTING

THE TENTH DAY OF ADVENT—GRANT SNYDER

1 Then Jesus was led up by the Spirit into the wilderness to be tempted by the devil. 2 And after fasting forty days and forty nights, he was hungry. 3 And the tempter came and said to him, "If you are the Son of God, command these stones to become loaves of bread." 4 But he answered, "It is written, 'Man shall not live by bread alone, but by every word that comes from the mouth of God'" (Matthew 4:1-4).

I recall so fondly the past family feast on Christmas Day around my grandmother's oak table. It was more of a "boat," really, that stretched impossibly far with all the leaves put in, and had to be angled in the dining room, from corner to corner, just to fit. She would stack the table with so much food that as a child I couldn't imagine how many people she must have expected. Then we'd gather, join hands and thank God together for such great bounty.

It's easy to be grateful around the holidays, when the food, gifts and fellowship seem without end. The idea of restraint where food is concerned seems contrary to how we celebrate the holidays. Food is everywhere, and seems etched in both our memories and our plans. A good meal is how many of us communicate our love to family and friends, toiling to make a memorable feast that we can enjoy and share. It seems that whenever the holidays approach, whenever we gather, food is a central theme.

Perhaps that's why this is a perfect season to reflect on the spiritual discipline of fasting. Though the Bible doesn't command Christians to fast, it is shown to be spiritually beneficial to us. In Acts, fasting was done prior to important decisions (Acts 13:2; 14:23). Also, in both the Old and New Testament, fasting is part of spiritual reflection accompanied by prayer (Psalm 69:10; Luke 5:33). In all these examples, fasting is a means to turn focus from the body to God, and ready ourselves to hear His voice in our lives.

Fasting is also an act of worship (Luke 2:36-37) and piety directed toward God (Matthew 6:16-18). Like all forms of worship, whether song, humility, praise or confession, it's the heart that matters. If in our fast, our emphasis continues to be on ourselves, in which we reflect on our suffering, our hunger or even weight loss, we have missed the point of verses like Matthew 6:16-18.

"And when you fast, do not look gloomy like the hypocrites, for they disfigure their faces that their fasting may be seen by others. Truly, I say to you, they have received their reward. But when you fast, anoint your head and wash your face, that your fasting may not be seen by others but by your Father who is in secret. And your Father who sees in secret will reward you."

Fasting, the way that Christ did, strips away the distraction of the body and affirms before God that He is fully master of our devotion and attention. We assert His primacy in our lives, and we pursue His ways, which magnificently transcend the preoccupations of our flesh. Fasting reminds us that there is nothing, even the very survival of our body, that stands as more important to us than God.

FAMILY DISCUSSION

- Fasting is generally associated with food, but denying ourselves anything temporarily to focus all our attention on God is a fast. What do you hear God asking you to give up temporarily in your own life to better focus on Him?
- In Matthew 6:16-18, Christ tells us to hide our fasting from others, and present it to God alone. Why do you think Christ tells us to do that? What is gained if others don't see our sacrifice?

PRAYER

Heavenly Father, Master of our lives, and King of all creation,

We admit before you now the many distractions that prevent us from seeing you, and hearing your voice. The world is a confusing place, and one that tests our commitment to you and your ways. Father, give us now the gift of sacrifice to you. Bless us with a heart of surrender before you, and help us to deny ourselves in full devotion to you. Bless us that our fast would not be impeded by our own suffering or pride. And give us your Holy Spirit that we may understand your will, and know your power in our lives.

In the name of your Son, Jesus Christ, Amen.

A WORK-LIFE THAT HONORS GOD

THE ELEVENTH DAY OF ADVENT—CYNDI SCHULENBURG

23 Whatever you do, work heartily, as for the Lord and not for men, 24 knowing that from the Lord you will receive the inheritance as your reward. You are serving the Lord Christ (Colossians 3:23-24).

One summer, when I was home from college on break, I got hired at Best Products, a department store. My job was to manage their 10-line phone system, greet customers and help answer any questions they might have. That same summer, our church was talking about how to share our faith. They had a contest to write a short, patriotic and inspirational essay on the subject of faith and our country. The winner's essay would be turned into a pamphlet and passed out to the church so they could share it with friends and co-workers over the Fourth of July holiday. Since I am extremely competitive and they mentioned the word "prize," of course I was going to enter. Never mind that I'm not really a writer and that the prize wasn't all that great.

I won the contest. So when the pamphlets were handed out, I started thinking about to whom I could give a copy. I took one to work with me at Best Products with the intention of starting small and only giving it to my boss. It turned out she was so excited for me that she put it on the all-staff bulletin board! She made a large sign with big black arrows that read, "You should read this! Your co-worker, Cyndi Burkett, wrote it and won a contest!" So much for starting small!

It has been years since that experience and the thing that still surprises me is what I didn't know at the time. Apparently, there had been a huge problem with theft at this particular store. So much in fact, that there was a secret internal investigation taking place. All of the employees were under surveillance and investigation. Our actions, relationships, time cards, work ethics and performance—even our conversations—were under scrutiny. I was observed and recorded in an effort to determine if I was a part of the ring of theft. In the end, it wasn't the reading of the pamphlet (my thoughts and words about Jesus) that determined if I was innocent. It was the investigation of my character (how I acted like Jesus) that proved I was innocent. I thought that the pamphlet was the tool that would bring my faith into my workplace. And, who knows what effect, if any, it had on those who read it. But, the bigger conduit for honoring God at work was in how I lived my life for Him. Whether we are aware or not, we are constantly being observed. Our verse for today reminds us that WHATEVER we do, we should do it for our true boss, the Lord. Your love for Jesus, lived out by your obedience to Him and the principles found in His word, is a powerful influence to those around you.

As you enter your workplace this Christmas season, pray that God's character would shine through you. Pray for your coworkers—that the blessing of knowing Him would be theirs. And thank Him that He has given you the opportunity to be influential for Him.

FAMILY DISCUSSION

- Who do you work with that needs the blessing and hope that you have through your relationship with Jesus?

- How does your love for God and His Word influence your behavior, attitudes and ethics when you are at work? Give an example.
- Since we are to reflect God's character, what verses can you find that speak about God's character?

PRAYER

Take some time to pray what is on your heart.

THE GIFT OF HEALING

THE TWELFTH DAY OF ADVENT—ALISA RABIN BELL

27 Now you are the body of Christ, and each one of you is a part of it. 28 And God has placed in the church first of all apostles, second prophets, third teachers, then miracles, then gifts of healing, of helping, of guidance, and of different kinds of tongues. 29 Are all apostles? Are all prophets? Are all teachers? Do all work miracles (1 Corinthians 12:27-29 - NIV)?

One of the best Christmas gifts we ever gave our daughter was a real sewing machine. The look on her face was precious. She was very surprised. But we learned quickly that there were a lot of parts to this machine—and if any one of them was slightly out of alignment, the machine wouldn't work. The same can be said of the human body. When our bodies are sick, broken or out of alignment, they don't function well either. We would later see firsthand the similarities between a piece of machinery and the human body.

This past spring, when the seasons changed, my husband decided to adjust the ceiling vents to help air flow in our house. He made the major error of improperly standing on a chair that couldn't support his weight. (He's a big guy.) The chair tipped and he fell, landing on his left shoulder. It was enough to send any normal person at least to the doctor, let alone the E.R. Not him. It took three months for him to finally decide to have the doctor check it out.

While at the appointment, he asked the doctor to also take a look at his right hip, which had been bothering him after a summer of playing soccer with our daughter. A staph infection when he was young plus years of semi-pro sports left him with a not-so-great hip that would probably need surgery one day. The end of the appointment left him with good news about his shoulder, but bad news about the hip. It was fractured, and he was sent straight to the E.R.

After five hours of MRIs and x-rays with doctors and nurses baffled by my husband's pain tolerance—he *walked* in with a fractured and severely arthritic hip—we were recommended to an orthopedic specialist. A full hip replacement was prescribed after the fracture healed.

One month later, at the age of 44, he had a full hip replacement. The successful surgery had him up and walking within a day, and home from the hospital three days later.

Here's where things took a strange turn. When he came out of his first rehab appointment a few days after getting home, he was sweating profusely and had trouble catching his breath. The rehab therapists were very worried about him and tested his blood oxygen level. We were all shocked to see how low it was. He was raced back to the E.R. I drove behind the ambulance in tears while my best friend prayed over the phone for us.

I was extremely scared as a dozen doctors and nurses hooked him up to every machine they had. Several hours later, we were told the complications weren't related to his hip, but his heart. His heart? What?! They moved him to the cardio-pulmonary I.C.U. What we learned next was a bit of a relief. He had cardio hypertrophic myopathy, which, in lay terms is a thickening of the heart's walls. It's hereditary, his mom had it and it's controllable with medication.

When we look at this *whole* story, we quickly realize that God had His hand on my husband and all of us throughout this situation. God healed him AND saved his life. Think about it . . . he fell off a chair and hurt his shoulder . . . went to the doctor to have it checked . . . needed a full hip replacement . . . then finally found out he had a heart condition, which resulted in measures to save his life.

For it is by grace you have been saved, through faith—and this is not from yourselves, it is the gift of God—not by works, so that no one can boast. For we are God's handiwork, created in Christ Jesus to do good works, which God prepared in advance for us to do (Ephesians 2:8-10).

We believe that God saved his life. It was truly a gift of healing. We are told in Jeremiah 29:11 that He has a plan for each of our lives. But He also tells us that when we call on Him and pray, He will listen to us and we will seek and find Him.

Like our daughter's Christmas sewing machine, the human body is incredibly complex and won't function when any parts are broken. God has given the body of Christ many gifts, including the gift of healing as revealed in 1 Corinthians 12:28. In James 5:13-16, we are told to pray for those who are sick and confess our sins to each other. This helps us make disciples who are focused on sharing their story and praying for healing for others.

Christmas gifts that we give to each other are nothing compared to the gifts that God has given us!

FAMILY DISCUSSION

- What is your testimony to God's healing power and how are you sharing it with others?
- How will you recognize and appreciate God's purpose for your life?
- How does the Christmas season help you see God's precious gifts in your life and the lives of others?

PRAYER

Dear Heavenly Father,

Thank you for the gift of healing. We pray that you continue to heal those in our congregation who are struggling with health issues, especially at this special time of year. We also recognize that not everyone is healed of their pains or illnesses in this life, but are when they are taken home to be with You. We are grateful to You for sending Your Son to die for our sins. His birth and sacrifice mean the world to us. Help us use our testimony to make more disciples for Jesus Christ.

In His Precious Name, Amen.

IMPACTING THE WORLD IN YOUR BACKYARD

THE THIRTEENTH DAY OF ADVENT—KARI BENNETT

8 "But you will receive power when the Holy Spirit comes on you; and you will be my witnesses in Jerusalem, and in all Judea and Samaria, and to the ends of the earth" (Acts 1:8)

As I drove my daughter home from small group one night, she broke into tears. After some conversation, I understood that her tears flowed because she didn't feel like she was doing anything of significance in her life. She "just" played sports. That's the way her youth group friends saw her—as a sports kid. We had watched a video during youth group about a high school student who was finding sponsors for kids through Compassion Ministries. She was having much success and making a difference in a lot of people's lives. That night, the girls shared something they were passionate about. When it was her turn, my daughter didn't know what to say. Her friends helped her out by saying, "sports." She felt like this wasn't a very important thing—especially compared to the girl in the video.

Do you ever feel like you are stuck in a role or location that is unimportant? Or, life is so busy with work, family and schedules that you don't spend time thinking about how you can advance the gospel? In these times, when we feel that our role is not significant, it's important to remember that God has a plan for each of us. Jeremiah 29:11 tells us, "'For I know the plans I have for you,' declares the Lord, 'plans to prosper you and not to harm you, plans to give you hope and a future'" (NIV). We are where we are because of God's divine plan. He gives us opportunities to reach people for the gospel right where we are—whether it's at a job, at home, in our neighborhood, at a Christmas gathering or even as part of a sports team. And while it's important for us to reach those in other countries with the gospel, it is equally important to reach those right in our own backyard with that life-saving message. God has great plans for us. If we pay attention, we will see the many opportunities He brings to us each day.

My daughter and I talked about the various people she can be an example to through sports. Whether it's through practicing good sportsmanship as an example to her teammates and the opposing team, accepting with grace the inevitable calls from officials that she disagrees with, respecting her coaches, inviting her teammates to youth group activities or even sharing the gospel with her teammates that don't know the Lord, God has her on that team for a reason. It's her job to pay attention to where she has been placed, look for opportunities to share Jesus with others and handle herself in a way that makes people notice that she is different because of her relationship with Jesus.

My son has had this opportunity through sports too. God allowed him to be part of the special teams unit on his high school football team. The coach responsible for this group is a believer. He knew the boys that were part of this small group were also believers. He encouraged the boys to take a knee at midfield and give thanks at the end of each game. He also encouraged them to invite their teammates and the opposing team to join them. What started in my son's freshman year as a small group of players has grown to include both teams taking a knee and praying after each game. My son is blessed to be part of this and often leads the post-game prayer. It's a great example of being a witness to not only teammates but parents, fans, officials and coaches. People have celebrated and been moved by this display of faith and sportsmanship. This is my son's backyard. It is a great example to his sister and to us of how we can be an influence to those God has put us in contact with—right in our own backyard.

FAMILY DISCUSSION

- Where might see opportunities to share the gospel, right where God has you?
- If you dream big, what is a God-sized opportunity that would be fun to do to advance the gospel? Don't let money, age, time or anything else be an issue—just think BIG!
- Will you commit to seeing the opportunities God brings to you in the next few weeks, then acting on them by being an example or sharing about Him?

PRAYER

Dear Lord,

Thank you that I can trust in your plan for my life. Thank you that you love me and know right where I am at. Help me to see the opportunities you give me daily to share about Jesus. Give me courage and the power of the Holy Spirit to take advantage of these opportunities to obey your command to make more disciples this Christmas season and throughout the entire year.

In Jesus' Name, Amen.

THE GIFT OF SABBATH

THE FOURTEENTH DAY OF ADVENT—JJ WESSMAN

8 "Remember the Sabbath day, to keep it holy" (Exodus 20:8).

To truly understand the Sabbath—or, in Hebrew, the Shabbat—we need to understand what it really is. In Exodus 20, we see that remembering the Shabbat is one of the 10 Commandments. But the amazing thing is that the Shabbat started in Genesis 2.

"Thus the heavens and the earth were finished, and all the host of them. And on the seventh day God finished his work that he had done, and he **rested** on the seventh day from all his work that he had done. So God blessed the seventh day and made it holy, because on it God **rested** from all his work that he had done in creation" (Genesis 2:1-3).

In this passage, it says God rested. The Hebrew word here is Shabbat, which means to cease or desist. So on the seventh day, God "shabbated"—He rested from the work of creating that He had done for six days. Not only did He rest but He set it apart. He made it holy. This set apart holy day in which one ceases and desists is the Jewish concept of the Shabbat, which runs from Friday at sundown to Saturday at sundown.

Now that we know what Shabbat is, the next question is how do we set it apart or remember it? Exodus 20:8 tell us that remembering the day will keep it holy, Exodus 20:11 tells us not to work and Isaiah 58:13 reminds us not to do our pleasure on Shabbat.

These directions for Shabbat are minimal but hold great significance to us as believers in Yeshua (Jesus). Who would like a day to "shabbat"—to cease or desist from all work? Who would like to rest like God rested after His creating? The Shabbat is a time to rest in God—to slow down, dare I say, stop, and set the day apart to focus on God.

Isaiah 58: 13-14 sums up greatly the blessing for those who follow the Shabbat.

"If you turn back your foot from the Sabbath, from doing your pleasure on my holy day, and call the Sabbath a delight and the holy day of the LORD honorable; if you honor it, not going your own ways, or seeking your own pleasure, or talking idly; then you shall take delight in the LORD, and I will make you ride on the heights of the earth; I will feed you with the heritage of Jacob your father, for the mouth of the LORD has spoken."

Remembering the Shabbat will slow us down after a very busy and hectic week, have us take time to focus on God and take delight in Him! Could you imagine riding on the heights of the earth?

FAMILY DISCUSSION

- How can we set apart the Shabbat and remember it?

PRAYER

Dear God,

As we set apart the Shabbat to rest in you, please cover us in your peace and give us rest that only you can bring. As we focus on you, draw us to you and into a better relationship with you as we focus on knowing you more. Thank you for your Shabbat rest!

In the name of Yeshua, Amen!

YOUR UNDENIABLE MISSION FIELD

THE FIFTEENTH DAY OF ADVENT—HOLLY PRICE

31 "The second is this: 'You shall love your neighbor as yourself.' There is no other commandment greater than these" (Mark 12:31).

Most Christians are excited to talk about our Heavenly Father with friends who are also Christians, but what about our neighbors? It is awkward to start those conversations, especially if we don't know where they stand. God placed each of us in a specific time and place, though, with unique gifts, and He calls us to make more disciples for Christ. Just as our careers can be a mission field, so can our neighborhoods.

As our church prepared for Easter two years ago, we went door-to-door in neighborhoods surrounding our church to invite people to our Easter service. I wondered what kind of reactions we might receive and I braced for negative ones. Our groups met back at church afterward and shared many beautiful stories of how God provided miracles that day. At one home, a mother and her daughter prayed that God would give them a clear sign, leading them to the church that He wanted them to attend, and that very morning they received a knock on their door. Our Lord works in beautiful and miraculous ways!

When I got back home I was compelled to knock on some doors in my own neighborhood. I wasn't sure where any of them stood in their faith, but I took that leap. All of the people I visited with welcomed me warmly. This simple act broke the ice to begin conversations about our faith. They were all members at various churches in the area, and I was overjoyed to know that my family was surrounded by many strong Christians. One of the neighbors in particular, Dana, has since become a prayer warrior with me. Before she moved in I had prayed that a Christian would live in that home, and my prayer was answered. During the same time, Dana had prayed that God would bless her with a good friend in the neighborhood. God answered her prayer as well.

It is easy to let the awkwardness of starting a conversation about our faith prevent us from knocking on those doors, but we forget that we might discover blessings upon blessings. It could be an opportunity to be a light to those needing it most—and possibly even be an answer to prayer.

FAMILY DISCUSSION

- Which neighbors would you consider inviting to church for Christmas?
- How have your neighbors been a blessing to you?
- How could you be a blessing to your neighbors during this Christmas season?

PRAYER

Dear Heavenly Father,

As we celebrate the birth of your precious Son, please open up our hearts to the needs of our neighbors. Please use us to bring others closer to you, to glorify you now and always.

In Jesus' name, Amen.

BE STILL AND KNOW

THE SIXTEENTH DAY OF ADVENT—DARRIN GEIER

10 "Be still, and know that I am God. I will be exalted among the nations, I will be exalted in the earth!" (Psalm 46:10)!

I was almost lost. I knew I could retrace the route I had taken, to eventually find myself back where I started. But I no longer was certain of my location on the map. And it was an exhilarating feeling! It was a chilly October afternoon. I had taken a few days off to escape, get away and spend some time mountain biking and camping. The Superior National Forest welcomed me that day with the blazing hues of autumn. I've always marveled at the beauty of this part of northern Minnesota. And that day, surrounded by bright yellow aspens and the sweet aroma of the boreal firs, I was spellbound!

I knew I had to stop and turn around. It would be dark in a couple of hours. But before backtracking the primitive forest roads I was traveling, I got off my bike and paused to take in my surroundings. At that moment, it occurred to me how utterly quiet it was. I marveled at the contrast to the busyness of job and tasks and duty back home. And miles back at my campground I was sure the tenants in the site next to mine were still busily running their RV's generator, banging pans and yelling at their dogs. But here, deep in the solitude of the woods, I had found something I desperately needed . . . silence. All I heard were the subtle whispers of creation—birds singing, leaves rustling and, as if to remind me that I was alive, my own heart pounding in my chest.

In the world I live in, noise is the rule and silence the exception. Deadlines dictate my schedule, advertising targets my attention and headlines remind me of the perils of this world. Even the best things in my life—family, church, relationships—place their own demands and compete for my time. And I can easily lose myself among the clangor of life's responsibilities and distractions. So when I found myself almost lost in the woods, it's no wonder I was startled by the silence.

The invitation to "be still" in Psalm 46 is cherished by many. These aren't difficult words to understand or accept, because we're all too aware of the frenzied pace of our lives. And there's just something welcoming about God's command to slow down. If you're like me, these words are met with a sense of relief as you're reminded of the permission—the mandate—to find God in the quiet. But for me, the lure of this invitation can also be mingled with a pang of guilt, a remorse in my soul. Because as much as I long for stillness, I'm so easily entrapped by the noise around me. It's hard to find time and space for silence in the chaos of everyday life.

Imagine what Mary's life was like after being visited by an angel and receiving the news that she would give birth to the Savior! Talk about chaos—her whole life was turned upside down! So what did she do next? She headed for the hills for some quiet time! Luke's Gospel tells us that Mary traveled to the hill country of Judea to spend a few months with her relative, Elizabeth. It was during this time that Mary found some much needed space for reflection. And we see Mary respond to God with a song of praise—*the Magnificat*—recorded in Luke 1:46-55. Her words are the obvious overflow of time spent with her creator. "My soul magnifies the Lord, and my spirit rejoices in God my Savior . . . "

As much as I would like to, I can't make room in my life for a four-day weekend in the woods very often. But there is good news. God offers his presence in the very midst of our everyday busyness. As we read the rest of Psalm 46, we're reminded that God is our "very present help in trouble" (Psalm 46:1). Let's not forget that God is here, right in the center of our chaos. The peace he offers is close at hand—and stillness is more available than we think. The spiritual discipline of silence can be practiced even amid our tumultuous everyday moments. We need simply to remember to "be still and know that he is God."

FAMILY DISCUSSION

- What are the everyday things that distract you or get in the way of finding silence? What's loud in your life?
- What practical things could you do to make more time for silence in your life? Make a list of ideas.
- How might this Christmas season be different if you more intentionally sought out quiet moments alone with God?

PRAYER

Dear God,

Thank you for being ever-present, even in the busyness and troubles of my life. Help me yearn for quiet moments with you. And in those moments, take away distractions, meet me where I am and help me listen well to your voice. I pray that this Christmas, you'll reveal to me a glimpse of the fullness of life that can be lived by those who are in tune with your Spirit, walking in your rhythms of grace and mercy.

In Jesus' name, Amen.

TO LOVE AN ENEMY

THE SEVENTEENTH DAY OF ADVENT—PETER AKINBORO

27 "But I say to you who hear, Love your enemies, do good to those who hate you, 28 bless those who curse you, pray for those who abuse you (Luke 6:27-28).

Growing up, I loved Christmas. I wanted to celebrate the holiday through December and January. I still love Christmas—the festive atmosphere, family get-togethers and sharing of gifts. Christmas is based on the greatest expression of love—the perfect, almighty God giving himself in the form of His son to dwell among His creation. Here, He reveals a perfect example of the kind of love He requires of us.

Loving those who love us is easy, but loving those who do not love us, or seek to do us harm, is the difficult part. It is one thing to profess our love for a hostile people, from afar, out of harm's reach. It is another to be willing to embrace them. Those who hate us, who curse and abuse us, are usually known to us—our neighbors. Hence, the command to love our neighbors, loved ones and enemies. The command to love is not just an obligation for us to obey. It is a command, because God designed us to need, give and receive love. We can't live without each other's love. It is how God moves among us—the mechanism of his presence (John 13: 34-14: 23). This makes us human. Without love we are just beings.

Those who need love the most are those we perceive lack love, that is, those who are hostile to us. Loving the way God showed us, He did not wait for us to ask. God gave his son as a ransom for those who are hostile to Him, and we have Christmastime as a reminder of this most generous loving kindness. Christmas is a good "excuse" to share love with those people who normally don't welcome us. There are many times when loving is easier said than done. If loving was meant to be easy, it would not have been a command. When it becomes difficult to love, we should do it because God commanded us to (John 13: 34-35). The Bible tells stories of love displayed in difficult moments: The Good Samaritan sacrificed in sharing love (Luke 10:30-37), David displayed great love in sparing the life of his enemy (1 Samuel 24: 1-7 and 26: 5-12), Joseph showed immense love for the brothers who sold him into slavery (Genesis 37-45) and Jesus prayed for the people that crucified him (Luke 23:34). This season, share love—particularly with people you consider enemies. And say a prayer for the unreachable.

FAMILY DISCUSSION

- Do you know anyone you need to tell about the reason for Christmas?
- Make a list of difficult people or situations in your life that need the love of God.
- Search out a unique display of love in the Bible and pray for the same for the world.

PRAYER

Dear Lord,

We know loving can be difficult sometimes. We also know that you are the source of love. Teach us to love, even when it is difficult. Show the world your love in our daily lives, leading them to you.

In Jesus' name, Amen.

CHOOSING LESS

THE EIGHTEENTH DAY OF ADVENT—DREW MATTISON

21 Jesus said to him, "If you would be perfect, go, sell what you possess and give to the poor, and you will have treasure in heaven; and come, follow me" (Matthew 19:21).

When I got married, my wife introduced me to a wonderful Christmas tradition that we have continued in our family with our children. We call this the Mary and Joseph meal. On Christmas Eve, we eat a very simple meal that Mary and Joseph could have eaten on their journey to Bethlehem that includes bread, cheese and dried fruits. We also eat the meal by candlelight and take time to pray together. During the Christmas season, there are many stresses that we all encounter: shopping for the perfect present, travelling across town or across the country, and large family gatherings. The Mary and Joseph meal helps us focus on the birth of Jesus, and celebrate His life and the life He gives each one of us.

Jesus desires for each of us to live lives full of satisfaction and fulfillment. The gift of Jesus that God gives us at Christmas is all the evidence we need to affirm this truth. When we embrace the gift of Jesus and allow his Spirit to dwell in us, it leads to unspeakable joy!

While God's desire for us to be satisfied encourages us, sometimes we try to fulfill that desire in ways that do not honor him. Jesus' command to the rich, young ruler to "go, sell what you possess and give to the poor" was His way of showing the misplaced desire in the rich, young ruler that focused on material wealth. The ruler did not want to sell his possessions because he clung to them—not Jesus—as the source of life.

God created each and every one of us with a warning system that tells us if we are living the life He desires to bless us with, or if we are beginning to follow our own way instead of His. With the rich, young ruler, Jesus invited him to sell his possessions and follow Him, but the invitation was rejected. Jesus knows that He is the only gift that can satisfy. Any other gift will not endure. But, the gift that is eternal will only continue to grow. We all clearly see the folly in the rich, young ruler and his foolishness. He wanted to keep his many possessions. He chose his possessions over Jesus, but the possessions did not satisfy. But, in our own lives we do not always see as clearly. We do not always see the idol we elevate over following Jesus. Jim Elliott, a missionary to Ecuador in the 1950s, summarizes this principle, saying "He is no fool who gives what he cannot keep to gain what he cannot lose." As we focus on the treasure in heaven that Jesus promises us as we follow Him, let us be a church that gives what we cannot keep.

FAMILY DISCUSSION

- What is your misplaced desire?
- What can you do to cling to the life that Jesus gives and reject temptation?
- How have you seen others in our community live courageously by following Jesus and rejecting society's definition of success?

PRAYER

Dear Jesus,

Show me my misplaced desire and help me trust you. I know that you invite me on a daily basis to follow you. While I celebrate your virgin birth during this Christmas season, I cannot help but think of the sacrifice that you gave on Good Friday. You gave the ultimate sacrifice that led to the ultimate life. I thank you for this gift. Help me reject any definition of success that leads me away from you. Help me reject the desire to control that suggests that I don't trust you to control. Help me reject the desire for lust that suggests I can be satisfied apart from you. Help me reject the need for worldly significance, because I am your child and significant in your eyes, and that is enough. Help me follow you.

In Jesus' name, Amen.

DISCIPLED THROUGH ADDICTION: A TESTIMONY

THE NINTEENTH DAY OF ADVENT—RICHARD MINETTE

13 No temptation has overtaken you that is not common to man. God is faithful, and he will not let you be tempted beyond your ability, but with the temptation he will also provide the way of escape, that you may be able to endure it. 14 Therefore, my beloved, flee from idolatry (1 Corinthians 10:13-14).

I have struggled with addiction my entire life. When my wife and I moved to Minnesota from Arizona nine years ago, I started having back pain, which required surgery. The pain after the operation was quite severe, so I was put on morphine and oxycodone. I enjoyed the feeling that these meds gave me so much. Before long, I was abusing them. I became addicted to opiates. Eventually I was using methadone and any and all opiates that I could find—including heroin. I was self-destructing and spiraling toward death.

My wife pleaded with me to get help, so I checked myself in to Hazelden for detox and treatment. I successfully completed treatment and was clean for almost two years. I even started the Addictions

Ministry at Woodbury Community Church, but *I* did not have any support from a sponsor or mentor and wasn't accountable to anyone but myself. I thought I was doing well until heroin crept back into my life and I relapsed. I was so full of shame that I could no longer attend church and, of course, was unable to continue the addictions ministry. How could I help anyone when I could no longer help myself? I felt I had let everyone down and just wanted to run away from everything. My addiction just kept getting worse. I went into isolation.

14 BUT EACH PERSON IS TEMPTED WHEN THEY ARE DRAGGED AWAY BY THEIR OWN EVIL DESIRE AND ENTICED. 15 THEN, AFTER DESIRE HAS CONCEIVED, IT GIVES BIRTH TO SIN; AND SIN, WHEN IT IS FULL-GROWN, GIVES BIRTH TO DEATH (JAMES 1:14-15 - NIV).

Heroin took my life. It became my idol or my god. I cannot even begin to describe how instantly heroin can get rid of physical or mental anguish. I snorted and shot up heroin daily for a year and a half. I completely withdrew from life and walked away from God. I *stopped* going to church—instead driving to North Minneapolis to pick up heroin while my wife was at church. I *stopped* listening to Christian music—choosing to listen instead to hard core metal regaling drug use. I *stopped* attending Bible studies—I preferred to be alone or with my heroin dealer. I *stopped* reading my devotionals and Bible and *stopped* communicating with my wife and church friends. My whole life (24 hours a day, seven days a week) revolved around getting and doing heroin.

At first, I loved it. I had found the ultimate high. But, when I realized that I was physically addicted and couldn't live without it, it was the scariest and most painful thing I have ever experienced in my life. My tolerance for the drug increased rapidly and my body craved larger amounts to maintain the high. I would start going into withdrawals within four hours of taking the drug. Going through withdrawals literally feels like you are dying. There are extreme sweats, shakes, chills, flu symptoms times 10, mental anguish and a desire to die. At my bottom, I wished I were dead, entertaining suicidal thoughts and actions by shooting up large amounts of heroin, hoping I wouldn't wake up. I realized that I couldn't live this way anymore. I was killing myself. I was non-existent in my relationships with the people I cared the most about—my Lord and Savior Jesus Christ, my wife, my children, my grandchildren and my real friends from church. I was depressed, ashamed and frightened at what I had become. I knew that I either had to quit or die.

I was afraid to quit because I knew how severe the withdrawals would be. They could possibly kill me. But I wanted a better way of living and longed for a relationship with God and those I loved again. I got down on my knees and begged God to help me quit heroin. My wife and pastor convinced me to get professional help. I prayed and prayed and finally surrendered! Jesus intervened. I believe it was a miracle. I voluntarily signed myself into Riverview Hospital to receive supervised detox and then went to Hazelden for treatment.

I have been clean for nine months now. There is hope for addiction. It is a disease that needs to be treated. Without treatment, it will eventually strip you of all good things in your life and eventually kill you. Today I am clean and sober. It's not always easy. The devil will always be there to tempt me. But, God is stronger than the devil.

1 I WAITED PATIENTLY FOR THE LORD AND HE TURNED TO ME AND HEARD MY CRY. 2 HE LIFTED ME OUT OF THE SLIMY PIT, OUT OF THE MUD AND MIRE; HE SET MY FEET ON A ROCK AND GAVE ME A FIRM PLACE TO STAND (PSALM 40:1-2 - NIV).

At first, I was extremely ashamed to walk back into church. I felt like the prodigal son, returning home to Woodbury Community Church. But I was welcomed back with open arms. WCC is an extremely loving church body. I need my church for love, support and accountability. I need to be accountable. I don't ever want to go into hiding and isolation again. I have a great support system. My pastor is one of my closest friends and my mentor. We meet weekly. My wife, who is my best friend, is a saint. She never left my side and never stopped praying for me. I have several very close church friends who stood beside me when I went for treatment. My Bible study never stopped praying for me. I attend a 12-step addictions group at Shepherd of the Valley Church. I put on the whole armor of God. I attend Alcoholics Anonymous/Narcotics Anonymous meetings weekly. I have a Christian sponsor. I read my devotions daily, pray always and listen to Christian music again. Most importantly I am walking daily with my Lord and Savior Jesus Christ again.

Philippians 4:13 says, "I can do all things through him who gives me strength" (NIV).

I would like to say to anyone suffering from addiction, of any kind, "Please surrender." The addiction will destroy everything in your life until you get help. First and foremost, you have to accept that you are an addict. Only *you* can admit that you are powerless over your addiction. Second, you must be *willing* to turn your life over to God and get help. And third, you must *accept* help and do whatever it takes to recover. God is good, and we have a very strong body of loving, accepting, caring Christian brother and sisters at WCC. You can beat your addiction one day at a time. I did! The devil lost—God won!

Seek the Lord with all your heart, all your soul and all your mind. I love my life today! I love Jesus today! I love my wife today! I love my children and grandchildren today! And, I love my WCC church family today! Thank you, Jesus! The chains are gone. I've been set free!

FAMILY DISCUSSION

- John 10:10 says, "The thief comes only to steal and kill and destroy. I came that they may have life and have it abundantly." How does this verse relate to Richard's testimony?
- Who are some people that we can be praying for God to set free?
- It's been said that we are all addicted to something. Is there something in your life that has too big a hold on your time, your resources or your heart?

PRAYER

Dear Jesus,

Thank you for the powerful testimony of your grace in the life of Richard. Thank you that because of the gift of Jesus, anyone can be set free from bondage to sin. Help me be a person of grace in this world. Help me have the eyes of Jesus to see the struggles that others go through. This Christmas season, come alongside all of those who are in the grips of addiction. Give them the courage to walk away from those things that hold them captive and into the freedom that can only come through you.

In Jesus' name, Amen.

CONFESSION IS GOOD FOR THE SOUL

THE TWENTIETH DAY OF ADVENT—MELANIE SNYDER

If we say that we have no sin, we are deceiving ourselves and the truth is not in us. If we confess our sins, He is faithful and righteous to forgive us our sins and to cleanse us from all unrighteousness. If we say that we have not sinned, we make Him a liar and His word is not in us (1 John 1:8-10).

These words of John remind us of the central role of confession in our lives. They show us the truth, not only of who we are, but of what we are to do about our sin. First, Verse 8 assures us that we cannot deny our sin, and doing so only leads to the great peril of self-deceit. To say we do not sin is to lie to ourselves, and further distance us from the truth. Denial of our sin has dire consequences, as Solomon warns in Proverbs 28:13: "He who conceals his transgressions will not prosper. . ." Further, as 1 John 1:10 shows, to deny our sin is to call Christ a liar as well, and to deny the impact of His word and the Spirit in our lives.

Our assurance is the promise of Christ's love and faithfulness, who not only died once and for all, for all sin, but who cleanses us personally upon our confession, and sets us on a path of righteousness (2 Chronicles 7:14; Luke 23:40-43). To live as human beings in the world is to confront the realities of what it means to occupy a dying body—We lurch ever onward toward death. Each day our bodies become more frail, and our days on this earth grow shorter. We are powerless to halt this progress toward physical death in the same way we are powerless to stop the consequences of our own sin. All have sinned, and all will do so again (Romans 3:10).

How magnificent to have a Father in Heaven who loves us in all our frailty, brokenness and rebellion that He alone stepped into our world in the person of Jesus Christ for the sole purpose of gathering us in righteousness unto Himself (Romans 6:23). Salvation was beyond our own grasp since we were born, and lived in sin. The birth of a baby at Bethlehem changed all of that.

More than 2,000 years ago, a star hung brightly in the sky above Bethlehem. This simple celestial event announced the entry of God, in the human flesh of Jesus Christ into the world. The prophecies that foretold the birth of Christ and His divine purpose are found throughout the Old Testament (Isaiah 7:14; Micah 5:1-2; Isaiah 11:1-10; Jeremiah 23:5). Jesus was born so He could deal, once and finally, with human sin. The whole of the nativity story is the beginning of the final chapter of man's struggle with sin, and God's perfect plan to restore us to Him. In that way, the confession of our sin is bound up in the Christmas story. When we stand before the manger and behold the gentleness and perfection of God's love (John 3:16), the confession of our sin is implicit if we believe that Christ was born the Son of God. Thus, by believing in Christ, in His deity and in the perfect purpose of His birth, we confess the truthfulness of our own sin before our Lord, who was born to suffer our penalty.

FAMILY DISCUSSION

- What do I see in the celebration of Christmas that distracts me from recognizing my own sin, and God's plan in Christ's birth?
- We think often of the sacrifices and offerings we make to God in our lives, yet none of those comes close to earning us salvation. How can confession of sin become a daily offering of our own humility and surrender to Christ?
- Think about the word "confess." It is used in the Bible to refer both to our statement of faith in Christ (Philippians 2:11), as well as our admission of sin (James 5:16). Both are imperative elements of our faith in Christ, and both share the fundamental aspect of "agreement." When we confess our faith in Christ, we agree that he is the Messiah, God among us, who has dominion and power over our lives. Likewise, we agree that our actions are sinful in confession. We agree that we have transgressed, and we agree that what God tells us in His Word is correct. Think about how seeing confession as "agreement" with God changes our perception of confession, and how it becomes a way of honoring God and offering ourselves to Him.

PRAYER

Our magnificent and holy Father,

We praise you for your perfect plan to redeem us through Jesus Christ. We praise you, and confess that you alone conquered our sin, and the penalty of that sin in our lives through the person of Jesus Christ. We confess our belief in the mission of Christ in this world, and His Lordship in our lives. And we confess our sin. We lay before you every broken piece of our lives, by which we have offended your will, and your ways. Thank you, Father, that you love us despite our failure. Thank you, God, for revealing the truth of our sin through your Word, and in our lives. Prepare our hearts, Lord, to confess to you all our sin, and to humble ourselves before you so you may heal us and use us for your glory.

In the name of your Son, Jesus Christ, Amen.

GOD'S HEART FOR THE WIDOW

THE TWENTY-FIRST DAY OF ADVENT—STEPHANIE WESSMAN

5 Father of the fatherless and protector of widows is God in his holy habitation (Psalm 68:5).

In the first verse of Psalm 68, David writes, "Let God arise, let His enemies be scattered . . . as smoke is driven . . . as wax melts before fire" (NASB). In Verse 4, he tells us that God rides on the clouds and in Verse 8, that the earth shakes and the heaven drops rain. Even Sinai itself is moved at His presence. These verses tell of God's power and might, His grandeur and splendor. He is deserving of praise! And then, nestled right in the middle of this awe-inspiring and fear-provoking description, where we truly get a picture that God is bigger than life, commanding men and weather and mountains, David slips.

"A father to the fatherless, a defender of widows, is God in His holy dwelling" (Psalm 68:5 - NIV).

What an amazing picture of God, great and mighty, able to vanquish enemies, call forth rain, use clouds as chariots, shaking the very earth, moving mountains—and yet He is also a father and defender of children and widows. What does this mean, that in His holy dwelling, the place that He is and exists, that He is a father to the fatherless and a defender of the widows?

It means that as much as it is true that His enemies must scatter as He arises, wherever there is a widow, He defends and steps in as a father for those who do not have one. Defending and protecting is at the essence of who God is as much as His might defines Him. The contrast is amazing, really. This juxtaposition of power and tenderness is truly breathtaking. It brings me to tears and humbles me to know that the one with so much power and grandeur sees the ones that have none. His holiness requires just action and He is their hope and salvation. It is so other—so unlike the human nature that tends to overlook and take advantage.

Repeatedly, God chastises Israel for oppressing and mistreating the widow (Ezekiel 22:7). His anger becomes aroused against them, for they neglected His command to not pervert the justice due the widow. They feel the weight of His curse (Deuteronomy 27:19) as they are attacked and exiled from their land. So what does this mean for us, His followers, His children? Caring for the widow is dear to God's heart. He is a God who loves His creation, each and every one. And since He created us in His image, we were made to care for the widow as well. God desires that we have His heart for the vulnerable, the forgotten and easily mistreated, those who have no voice of their own. The widows in our midst are actually our opportunity to be God-like, demonstrating His love and compassion, His defender's character to a fallen, lost world.

FAMILY DISCUSSION

- How do we do this? James 1:26 tells us to visit widows in their trouble. Job 31:18 tells us that Job reared the fatherless and guided the widow. In Isaiah 1:17 we are told to plead the case or fight the fight of the widow. What we need is time with God to acquire His heart and time with widows to know their needs. Visit a widow you know or invite her and her children over. Get involved as God shows you a need.

PRAYER

Dear Lord,

Give us your eyes to see the widows in our midst. Give us your heart for them. We pray for the widows and their children, that you'll bless them. Give us opportunities to reach out to those who are vulnerable, forgotten, mistreated, and to those who have no voice of their own. Thank you for being a God as rich in compassion as you are in might.

In Jesus' name, Amen.

HOW BIBLICAL HOSPITALITY COULD CHANGE THE WORLD

THE TWENTY-SECOND DAY OF ADVENT—TAMMIE HAVEMAN

9 Show hospitality to one another without grumbling (1 Peter 4:9).

I vividly remember the moment the nativity story came to life for me. I was 10-years-old and languishing through a midnight Christmas service. My exasperated mother had just roundly disciplined me for provoking my brother. And I wasn't paying a lick of attention to the service.

My little legs bounced impatiently, my Christmas dress scratched at my neck and my eyes drifted across the candle-lit sanctuary searching for something interesting to entertain my mind. I noticed my pastor pacing up front. And I found myself leaning in to listen as he began narrating a harrowing tale of the holy family's journey to Bethlehem. With dramatic effect, he described a weary Mary, suffering through back-breaking pain. He portrayed a stoic Joseph, trying to protect his beloved. And he condemned a town full of people who turned a pregnant mother away.

I followed along with rapt attention as he described the pungent smell of the barn, the animals lowing and how these base conditions were the only choice for the holy family because there was no room at the inn. I hadn't considered how smelly the barn would be until that moment in my life. And the effect was not lost on a young girl who spent copious amounts of time on her grandparents' pig farm.

I flopped back against my seat and stifled a horrified gasp that anyone would turn away a pregnant mother and force her to have a baby in a barn—particularly when she was carrying the Savior of the world. And my indignation at the callous innkeeper and heartless residents of Bethlehem seared itself into my mind for years to come.

"And she gave birth to her firstborn son and wrapped him in swaddling cloths and laid him in a manger, because there was no place for them in the inn" (Luke 2:7).

Anyone familiar with the nativity story could tell you that Jesus was born in the stable because there was no room for the family in the inn. Historians would add that inns in ancient times were undesirable and a last resort for any respectable family. So the fact that Joseph sought shelter at an inn indicates that the family's relatives and other townspeople had also turned them away. It is understandable to inject an undercurrent of censure toward the residents of Bethlehem whenever the nativity story is told. Because it's hard to fathom house after house rejecting a pregnant mother in such dire straits.

But what if we looked at the story from a different angle? In fact, what if we were invited to *admire* and even *emulate* the townspeople and the innkeeper? Bethlehem was overrun with people complying with the mandatory census. And in ancient times, hospitality was ingrained in the culture. It was common and even expected for families to house travelers and strangers. So we can assume that there was no room for the holy family anywhere because the townspeople were already being hospitable.

The residents of the area had filled their homes to the brim with sojourners and relatives. And bless that innkeeper, whomever he was. Because he offered a desperate couple the last bit of space he had available. So there is much to admire about this town and a culture in which hospitality was simply a way of life. And God used this common practice of hospitality as a tool for the spread of the gospel.

When Jesus commissioned the disciples to tell everyone about the Kingdom of God and to heal the sick, he instructed them in Luke 9, "Take nothing for your journey. Don't take a walking stick, a traveler's bag, food, money, or even a change of clothes. Wherever you go, stay in the same house until you leave town." Jesus sent out a ragamuffin group with no food, no money or even a spare tunic to tell people about the Kingdom. There was no Facebook or text message to alert anyone in the surrounding towns that that they were coming. There was no Homeaway.com or Expedia to book accommodations. Yet the disciples had every reason to expect that they would find families ready, willing and able to welcome them into their homes.

Hospitality was inherent to the spread of the gospel, not only during Jesus' time on earth but also as the early church grew. We find countless examples in Acts as well as throughout the epistles of generous hospitality being shown to missionaries and sojourners. And the countless saints who opened their doors for the sake of the gospel changed the world in the process. It might feel a little radical to modern-day believers to imagine opening our doors to strangers. But God clearly directs us to continue this practice as committed Christ followers. "Show hospitality to one another without grumbling" (1 Peter 4:9).

God designed our homes to be places of refreshment for saints as well as spaces of hope and truth for sinners. He directs us to welcome and show radical love to the stranger in our midst. And he clearly intends for us to use our homes generously to share his love. So perhaps we should be a little more like the townspeople, opening our doors to weary souls. We all should follow the example of the innkeeper, offering the last bit of space we have available to someone in need. And we all should pray for God to use our homes today like He did in ancient times, to continue changing the world for His glory.

FAMILY DISCUSSION

- In what ways have we shown hospitality to others as a family?
- How can we ensure that our home is ready to receive any unexpected guests God sends our way?
- What are some ways our family can use our home to offer rest and refreshment to friends and strangers?

PRAYER

Dear God,

I am grateful for the blessing of my home. Please give me opportunity to use it for the spread of the gospel. I welcome the stranger, the saint, the souls you send my way for refreshment and rest. May it be for your glory that I open my door.

In your name, Amen.

SPIRITUAL ORPHANS

THE TWENTY-THIRD DAY OF ADVENT—JASON NYGREN

27 Religion that is pure and undefiled before God the Father is this: to visit orphans and widows in their affliction, and to keep oneself unstained from the world (James 1:27).

Sometimes, it can feel like a battle.

At least that's how I felt when I started my first job in ministry. I was working in youth ministry with 20 students, none of whom had any experience being in a church and none from believing families. I didn't know exactly how difficult it was going to be until I was in the middle of teaching my first lesson. I was talking about the importance of trusting in God and trusting He will provide. When I mentioned the story of Abraham and Isaac I was met with blank stares. It was then that I knew I had to change the way I was communicating with them if I wanted our youth ministry to make an impact. And it was difficult. There were times when I wanted to throw my hands in the air and give up. Times when I watched as the influences in their life pulled them away from the God I was watching them discover. It can feel like one step forward and a few hundred back.

And that's ok.

Because this life is messy. It isn't our job to "fix" anyone. It isn't our responsibility to bury them in doctrine and rules only to show disappointment when they don't live up to our standards. We are called to love them with the same love that Christ loves us. That is a love with an infinite amount of grace and forgiveness. That doesn't mean we don't speak truth into their lives and that we encourage and enable decisions that lead them to walk away from God. So how do we walk this line? I believe Jesus answers this question for us in John 5:19-24.

"Jesus gave them this answer: 'Very truly I tell you, the Son can do nothing by himself; he can do only what he sees his Father doing, because whatever the Father does the Son also does. For the Father loves the Son and shows him all he does. Yes, and he will show him even greater works than these, so that you will be amazed. For just as the Father raises the dead and gives them life, even so the Son gives life to whom he is pleased to give it. Moreover, the Father judges no one, but has entrusted all judgment to the Son, that all may honor the Son just as they honor the Father. Whoever does not honor the Son does not honor the Father, who sent him. Very truly I tell you, whoever hears my word and believes him who sent me has eternal life and will not be judged but has crossed over from death to life'" (NIV).

Jesus is telling His disciples and, by extension, us, that we must seek after God in all we do. God loves each of us, and when we seek out His will, the Holy Spirit will stir in our hearts. He will speak to us and show us the times to be gentle, the times to share truth, the times to listen and the times to speak.

So this Christmas season, whether it is inviting your child's friend who comes from an unchurched home to dinner or going out to lunch with a co-worker whose family and friends discourage their faith and tries to pull them away, we can do these things.

Show love, not judgement. It isn't our place to judge others. It is our job to shower them with love. To encourage them. To listen to their stories. We show them Christ's love when we validate their struggles and tell them it is OK to question God. Remember that it is God who changes hearts, not us.

Don't demean and belittle their families. It can be very easy to blame someone's family and encourage that person to walk away. But we cannot punish parents, siblings and friends for not being followers of Jesus. We cannot hold them to the standards of a life they have not chosen to lead. We can speak truth into their lives when their friends and family lead them astray, but making the ones they love into enemies is not the answer.

Speak truth while showing more grace than condemnation. God calls us to speak His truth. In the great commission, Jesus tells us to make disciples and teach them all He has taught us. But He has also called us to speak truth while not creating guilt and fear. Let God work in the midst of truth and grace and see His Word thrive.

FAMILY DISCUSSION

- Who are the spiritual orphans in your life?
- Read John 5:19-47. What is Jesus telling us? How do we take this lesson into our interactions with those who don't have a faith background or family support for their faith?
- During this Christmas season, how can you show the love of Christ to the orphans in your life?

PRAYER

God,

In this Christmas season, let me see the spiritual orphans you have strategically placed in my life. Use me to accomplish your purpose, to show Your love, truth and grace. Please help me know when the Holy Spirit is calling me to speak and to listen. Above all else, let me reflect you.

In Jesus' Name, Amen.

SELF-EXAMINATION

THE TWENTY-FOURTH DAY OF ADVENT—JOE DELLARIA

23 Search me, O God, and know my heart! Try me and know my thoughts! 24 And see if there be any grievous way in me, and lead me in the way everlasting (Psalm 139:23-24)!

Whenever it was our turn to host Christmas when I was growing up, I knew one thing for sure—the house was going to be spotless before the guests arrived. This meant I had to clean my room and all the messes from my ongoing projects. I always wondered, "What's the big deal?"

Now, after raising my own family, I get it. You want to put your best foot forward and you want guests to feel welcome and comfortable when they arrive at your front door. In addition, by cleaning and preparing in advance, I find that I can relax and enjoy my guests more fully. This passage is about cleaning up your "spiritual house" before Jesus arrives on Christmas day.

The Psalm starts with the idea that God knows everything we do and think before we do (Verses 1-6). Verses 7-12 tell us that we cannot hide from God. Wherever we go, he is there. This is another acknowledgement that God knows everything about everyone. Verses 13-16 point out that God made us—again, he knows everything about us. Verses 17-18 speak of how the psalmist highly values God's thoughts. Then the psalmist states his hatred for the wicked, calling God to slay them (Verses 18-22). Evil people say one thing and mean or do another. They lie and manipulate. The psalmist's hatred for the wicked and their behavior sets the tone for the beginning of today's passage.

23a "Search me, O God, and know my heart!"
"Search me, O God" is the psalmist inviting God to search through every corner of his heart. Why would he do that? Because the psalmist doesn't want to be self-deceived like the wicked. All people are prone to self-deception and blind spots (Jeremiah 17:9; 1 Corinthians 4:4; I John 1:8, 10; Galatians 6:3; Proverbs 16:2; Proverbs 21:1 -2; Psalm 19:12; and Psalm 36:2). The best strategy to thwart self-deception is to allow God to tell us the truth about what is in our hearts. Those who sincerely invite God to search their hearts will get a full report—including the good and the bad. God will look at everything and encourage us where we are doing well *and* show us what needs to be cleaned up.

23b "Try me and know my thoughts!"
The best way to confirm what is really in one's heart is to do a test. If God asks you to do something, and you don't do it, you have failed the test. It shows that you don't trust or believe God, or you refuse to follow his direction. In the end, it means you don't fully love Jesus. Four times in John 14 and 15, Jesus said something along the lines of, "If you love me, you will obey me" (John 14:15, 14:21, 14:23 and 15:10). This is an invitation for God to test us.

24a "And see if there be any grievous way in me,"
This is a call for God to specifically show you what things are in your heart that are keeping you from being in full relationship with God. Unconfessed sin, even as a Christian, disrupts our relationship with God and separates us from him (James 4:4, John 9:31, Isaiah 59:2 and Psalm 66:18). We should desire to know every unknown sin in our hearts, as the psalmist does, so that we can confess, repent and be restored to a full and right relationship with God.

24b "and lead me in the way everlasting!"
This is the grand finale. The psalmist is choosing to yield his will to God. He is stating his desire to follow God fully. This is the key to a full relationship with God. We could never do this with our own strength. It is only when we fully yield to God, calling on Him to work in and through us, that we can be obedient. Jesus showed us how to do this—so we know we can do it too.

The point of the passage is that we must truly seek to know all sin that stands between us and God. Doing a full inventory is the only way to know what is in our hearts. It's kind of scary to make this invitation. But one thing we know—there is nothing better than living in full relationship with God. Only this can bring true peace, joy and satisfaction.

If you are wondering about identifying every sin, don't worry too much about that. Read 1 John 1:9. "If we confess our sins, he is faithful and just to forgive us our sins and to cleanse us from all unrighteousness." If we sincerely and genuinely seek to confess and repent of sin in our lives, God rounds to 100 percent, forgives and cleanses us of "all unrighteousness." I find that relieving and hope you do, too. The reason to do this is so that every Christian can have full relationship with God as we remember and celebrate Jesus' birth and what that means to us as Christians. Those who take this admonition to heart and do this will experience the full depth and breadth of their relationship with God!

FAMILY DISCUSSION

- How does inviting God to show you your sin make you feel?
- What do you think it will feel like if you do what Psalm 139:23-34 is calling you to do?
- Are you willing to do that so you can experience a full relationship with God?

PRAYER

Dear Heavenly Father,

I acknowledge that I have sinned and that I may not even remember or recognize the full extent of sin in my life. I know that these sins stand between you and me. I call on you to show me my sin and give me the strength and courage to confess and repent of everything you bring to mind. I claim your promise to "forgive me of all unrighteousness" and look forward to fully experiencing your love as you wash me of all my sins. Thank you for helping me draw nearer to you.

In Jesus' name, Amen.

LOVING SOCIETY'S THROWAWAYS

THE TWENTY-FIFTH DAY OF ADVENT—GRANT SNYDER

36 "I was naked and you clothed me, I was sick and you visited me, I was in prison and you came to me." 37 Then the righteous will answer him, saying, "Lord, when did we see you hungry and feed you, or thirsty and give you drink? 38 And when did we see you a stranger and welcome you, or naked and clothe you? 39 And when did we see you sick or in prison and visit you?" 40 And the King will answer them, "Truly, I say to you, as you did it to one of the least of these my brothers, you did it to me" (Matthew 25:36-40).

4 they said to him, "Teacher, this woman has been caught in the act of adultery. 5 Now in the Law, Moses commanded us to stone such women. So what do you say?" 6 This they said to test him, that they might have some charge to bring against him. Jesus bent down and wrote with his finger on the ground. 7 And as they continued to ask him, he stood up and said to them, "Let him who is without sin among you be the first to throw a stone at her." 8 And once more he bent down and wrote on the ground.

9 But when they heard it, they went away one by one, beginning with the older ones, and Jesus was left alone with the woman standing before him. 10 Jesus stood up and said to her, "Woman, where are they? Has no one condemned you?" 11 She said, "No one, Lord." And Jesus said, "Neither do I condemn you; go, and from now on sin no more." (John 8:4-11).

Once again, we are beset by the miracles of Christmas. Everywhere we turn, it seems we are embedded in the season with its carnival of color, light and sound, the familiar din of Christmas songs, cherished hymns of praise, our busyness and expectation. Our pace seems to increase and our tasks are never done. We hang decorations. Adornments. Things of beauty that shine, sparkle and glow. It's new and familiar at the same instant, able to rapture us to joyous times past, and hopeful days ahead.

This season is set apart in the year, both by our experience of it in the world, and our experience of it as Christians. It's a time that reminds us first and foremost how easy it is fall in love with the beauty that God has made—Beauty captured in the smiles and enthusiasm around us, beloved ritual and celebration and the depth of winter.

Amid that beauty, behind the lights, dimmed in the shadow of shiny things, there remains a forgotten people. They are cast aside, driven past and turned away. They are those who have been thrown out. They are easy to spot. There! Ahead on the skyway, sidewalk or mall. Moving toward me. A curt smile may do it, or brief nod that says, "I see you. I'm busy." They look like they will talk to me—or worse—expect something from me. "I'm not that guy. Not today. Besides—insert your favorite excuse here—"My family's waiting." "I've only got a few minutes." "This is an important call." "I don't have any change, or time or patience." "I'm filled up, overwrought, fed up, tapped out." "Busy." In the end, we surrender to the fact that today just isn't the day, and check our phone, send a text, read an email. Avert our path. It's Christmas, and there's stuff to do. I can lose myself, and my guilt in something . . . over there.

I think our regard for people—the true, honest, bare-bones measure of their actual importance in our lives—how we appraise their value—can be summed up by how much of an interruption we allow them to be in our day. Think about that. In Luke 12:34, Christ reminds us, "For where your treasure is, there your heart will be also." And in the verse that immediately precedes it, we hear Christ assuring us that to sell our possessions, to abandon the things of value in this world to the charity of others, is the first step toward a treasure that no thief can steal, and no moth can destroy.

What is that we are to treasure? Where should we find our heart? As we read above, in John 8:4-11, we see where Christ's treasure was in the way He responded to the "throwaways" of the first century. He stopped His day for them. Defended them. Taught them. Fed them, ate with them, prayed for them, forgave them. He was born for them, and then he died for them. When the Pharisees brought the woman forth to stone her, she was a pawn in their scheme against Christ. She was a throwaway—unworthy, unimportant, quick to be sacrificed to higher plans. On that day, in that moment, for that woman, Christ stopped the accusers, exposed their sin and sent them away. The woman left too, being assured by Christ not of her blamelessness, but of her worth. Though the rest of the world would cast her out, throw her away, Christ would not. His treasure was to mirror the radiance of His Father's love for a fallen world, and a condemned people. Where will our treasure be this Christmas? Who waits for us to stand before the crowd of accusers, and send them off?

FAMILY DISCUSSION

- If we desire to live like Christ, to be His disciples in this world, how can we mirror Christ's commitment to the throwaways of this world, or our country, or our community this season?
- Where do I see those who are throwaways in my daily life?

PRAYER

Heavenly Father,

Thank you! For all the experiences you allow us, for all the gifts you provide, for all the lessons you teach us, we thank you. I pray this day for those who walk among us, forgotten, cast out, rejected. I pray for a heart that weeps with them, and sees hope in their darkness and struggle. I ask that you watch over all your children, and bless me to cherish them as you do. I ask that you would open my eyes to suffering around me, open my arms that I may receive others in my life, as you've received me, and open my hands that I may carry their burden. Give me strength to meet the task before me, Lord. All praise and glory be to You.

In the name of Your Holy Son, Jesus Christ, Amen.

A HEART OF GRATITUDE

THE TWENTY-SIXTH DAY OF ADVENT—SHANE MCNAMARA

18 Give thanks in all circumstances; for this is the will of God in Christ Jesus for you (1 Thessalonians 5:18).

"'Tis the season," as they say—the season for thankfulness and to pursue peace on earth. We hear it all the time—in popular choruses and from people passing on the street— "peace on earth." Sometimes, though, there isn't peace, only agony and heartache. If we're honest, we all feel this way at some point. We wonder, "Where is this peace the angels promised us in Luke 2:14 when talking to the shepherds?"

Clearly, we know that peace on earth is not required for one to be grateful. Furthermore, we all probably know people who have been grateful in circumstances that made it seem they should have nothing for which to be grateful. Yet all too often that doesn't make it any easier for us to be grateful in the midst of terrible tragedy. No, we can't just see others' gratefulness and learn to be grateful. We need to know where it comes from.

Our gratefulness comes from that old refrain from Luke when the angels say, "Glory to God in the highest, and on earth peace to men on whom his favor rests." However, to fully understand this peace, we need to go back to when we lost our peace. We need to go back to creation, to the fall of man in Genesis 3. The Lord laid out the punishment for the first sin, cursing man, woman and the whole earth. We originally lost our peace because of Adam's sin. Today we continue to lose our peace because of our own sin. Please understand that all pain and suffering in this world has its origins in sin, directly or indirectly.

"All have sinned and fall short of the glory of God." This is the painful truth Paul lays out before us in Romans 3:23. When we understand that we have sinned and that our sin has brought a just punishment upon us, we know we deserve to suffer—and not just for a while, but eternally.

But praise be to God our Father, and our Lord Jesus Christ, that we have been spared. God has created a way for us to be reconciled to Him through our Savior, Jesus, who paid the price for our sin. When we believe in the name of Jesus, we are saved from the eternal punishment we so rightly deserve. If for no other reason, we ought to be grateful in everything because of this truth alone.

Yet, the Lord has gone beyond simply saving us from eternal suffering. He has given us His Spirit today. Every day we wake up and we know God's mercy has not run out, even in the most difficult times. I understand that even though we know this truth, it can be hard to be grateful when loved ones die, if you've just lost your job or in myriad other painful situations. In those moments, it is OK to cry out to God in sorrow and anger—just remember His mercies and allow Him to work. We were never promised an escape from pain in this life, but we have been promised everlasting life with an amazing God. Keep your focus on Him and you will have gratefulness to spare.

FAMILY DISCUSSION

- What is making it hard for you to be grateful?
- What are some blessings the Lord has poured out on you this week?
- Why is it important to remain grateful even in the midst of trials?

PRAYER

Jesus,

Thank you for coming to earth to reconcile me to God. I am forever indebted to you because of your great love. I know you have told us that there will be trials, and sometimes they are too much for me to bear. Please stand by me and give me your comfort. Help me remember all your blessings and remain grateful in all that I do.

Amen.

GOD'S HEART FOR THE OPPRESSED

THE TWENTY-SEVENTH DAY OF ADVENT—JOE DELLARIA

7 But the Lord sits enthroned forever; he has established his throne for justice, 8 and he judges the world with righteousness; he judges the peoples with uprightness. 9 The Lord is a stronghold for the oppressed, a stronghold in times of trouble. 10 And those who know your name put their trust in you, for you, O Lord, have not forsaken those who seek you (Psalm 9:7-10).

19 Go therefore and make disciples of all nations, baptizing them in the name of the Father and of the Son and of the Holy Spirit, 20 teaching them to observe all that I have commanded you. And behold, I am with you always, to the end of the age (Matthew 28:19-20).

Three definitions are helpful in understanding this Psalm.

>Oppressed: a person or people who are under oppression

> Oppression: to subject a person or people to undue burdens or exercise of authority; tyranny, despotism, and persecution are helpful synonyms
> Stronghold: security and protection in a high, safe place of retreat

Verses 1-6 of Psalm 9 contrast God's goodness and care with the temporary evil that wicked people force on the oppressed. We learn that God will punish and remove the wicked. This sets up our passage in Verses 7-10. Here we learn several things about God's character and being.

God is:

- eternally just and righteous, and judges with uprightness (Verses 7-8)
- a stronghold for the oppressed in their time of need (Verse 9)
- trustworthy because he won't forsake those who are oppressed and who call on him (Verse 10)

God is a stronghold for all of his followers (Psalm 18:2, Psalm 27:1, Psalm 37:9 and Psalm 144:2), but especially for the oppressed who call out to him. As a follower of Jesus, I seek to have God's character. If God is a stronghold to the oppressed, then I should be as well. God calls all of his followers to care for the oppressed by protecting them when they are unable to protect themselves.

Now we need to bring in today's second passage, Matthew 28:19-20. It is referred to as the Great Commission. These were Jesus' last words before ascending into heaven. You can see that the Matthew passage has the following verbs: go, make (disciples), baptize, teach. All of these are imperatives, or commands. This means Christ-followers are supposed to do these activities. English conceals an interesting feature of this passage. In Greek, the original language, there is only one imperative verb—"make disciples." The verbs go, baptize and teach only tell us how specifically to carry out the true focus of the passage—

which is to "make disciples!"

Jesus tells his disciples to "make disciples of all nations." That means regardless of sex, nationality, status or anything else, Jesus wanted all to be his disciples. This includes those who are oppressed.

For most of us, me included, this brings up a problem. Living in suburban America does not lead to convenient overlap with those who are oppressed. That is only half the problem. The other half is my busy life, which is packed with good things that leave little or no margin to respond if I did meet an oppressed person. This may be my greatest problem.

It sounds like there is an impasse between what God is calling us to do and our ability to obey. Not to worry, remember in Ephesians 2:10 God tells us, "For we are his workmanship, created in Christ Jesus for good works, which God prepared beforehand, that we should walk in them (Ephesians 2:10).
God has already prepared the good works he intends for us to do. All we need to do is ask for guidance, be open to obeying and be available. God will bring the person or people into our lives. To be prepared, I need to create margin in my life so I can respond. I also need to prepare by asking God to open my eyes and bring these people into my life. Finally, I need to live expectantly that God will do this.

In your mind, you have to make a decision whether you will carry out God's call no matter the cost. One of the things I have learned in my walk with Jesus is that whenever Jesus calls me to do something, he always provides what is needed. "Now to him who is able to do far more abundantly than all that we ask or think, according to the power at work within us" (Ephesians 3:20).
Are you willing to believe and act on God's promise found in Ephesians 3:20? If you are, then you are ready to act regardless of the cost to protect and disciple the oppressed. Just as Jesus did!

FAMILY DISCUSSION

- Whom do you know that is oppressed and needs discipling?
- If you know someone, will you act in faith and seek to disciple the person regardless of the cost? Will you trust that God will provide whatever is needed? What do you need to do to begin the process?
- If you don't know someone like this, will you pray that God will lead you to an oppressed person? Are you willing to serve as "God's stronghold" to meet the needs of this person (or people) and disciple them? What would that take?

PRAYER

Dear Heavenly Father,

You have blessed us abundantly with time, talent and treasure. These are yours. Help me use these to serve your kingdom and help it grow. Give me a heart of compassion for the oppressed. Show me someone I can be a stronghold for, and help me disciple them. I call on you to give me strength, wisdom and perseverance to complete the work you give me. May you get all the glory and honor as I serve obediently to further your kingdom.

In Jesus' name, Amen.

THE DISCIPLINE OF CELEBRATION

THE TWENTY-EIGHTH DAY OF ADVENT—LIZ NELSON

"4 Rejoice in the Lord always; again I will say, rejoice" (Philippians 4:4)!

"I have told you this so that my joy may be in you and that your joy may be complete" (John 15:11 - NIV).

The Christmas season is my favorite time of year. I have so many joyful memories of the holiday. As a kid, I would awake early in the morning and wait anxiously to unwrap the gifts that had been sitting under the tree all month long. I loved listening to my grandpa read from the Bible each Christmas and share a wise insight from the passage. In college, I would check my mail every day, waiting for the ornament my parents would send me. As I moved into my first apartment, I arranged my furniture based on where the Christmas tree would be placed—that's how much I really like Christmas! Looking back on all my good memories of family and church celebrations, I am reminded of the joyful celebrations that surrounded that first Christmas.

We are indeed in a season of celebration as we remember Jesus' birth. Although some people see Christmas as merely an excuse to get off work, this celebration is so much more! It invites us to join in God's joy by remembering His goodness and faithfulness. All too often, however, we allow that joy to be overcome by over-commitment, worry, sadness, stress and frustration. But these feelings are the very reasons why times of celebration are so important, especially to our spiritual lives.

If we need an example of a life lived in joy, we need to look no further than the life of Jesus. He attended weddings and took time to bless little children. He raised people from the dead and broke bread with the disciples. Here's good news for you. That joy can be ours as well! Jesus tells us that we need to remain in His love in John 15. In Verse 11, he says, "I have told you this so that my joy may be in you and that your joy may be complete." Likewise, the apostle Paul tells us that we can live in a state of perpetual joy. He writes in Philippians 4:4, "Rejoice in the Lord always. Again I say rejoice!"

Joy and happiness are not the same, however. Happiness is an emotion most often based on our circumstances. Joy runs deeper. It finds its source in God's goodness and faithfulness. This holiday season for many is a difficult time due to lost loved ones, failed relationships and financial difficulties, but we can still find the joy of Christ even in the midst of despair, hurt, struggle and loneliness. If this is where you find yourself this Christmas, remember that he doesn't want us to live humdrum lives, carrying these heavy burdens on our own shoulders. He wants us to live lives of joy and celebration.

How do we do this? How do we live lives of joy when we are constantly in the midst of the daily battles of life? By "casting all your care upon him, for he cares for you" (1 Peter 5:7 - NKJV). We need to take God at His word, that he can and will carry our burdens for us. That is the reason Jesus came as a baby that first Christmas, so that he might be our Savior not only in eternity but today as well. Our salvation doesn't begin the day we die but the moment we trust Christ as our Savior. That is the best reason for joyful celebration. While it is good to find joy in gift-giving and family get-togethers, joy is something that we must find not just on holidays, but also in our relationships with God—EVERY DAY!

FAMILY DISCUSSION

- What is the difference between happiness and joy?
- How will you find joy today and every day?
- What are your burdens this Christmas season? Will you let God take them away?

PRAYER

Dear Lord,

Thank you that you carry my burdens and hurts. Please help me joyfully celebrate your birthday this year and remember to celebrate you each day thereafter.

Amen.

DIVINE APPOINTMENTS

THE TWENTY-NINTH DAY OF ADVENT—BRIAN SCHULENBURG

30 So Philip ran to him and heard him reading Isaiah the prophet and asked, "Do you understand what you are reading?" 31 And he said, "How can I, unless someone guides me?" And he invited Philip to come up and sit with him (Acts 8:30-31).

Merry Christmas!

Today marks the end of our 30-day spiritual adventure. I hope that you have been blessed as you read this book each day.

As you celebrate with your family today, may you rejoice in the greatest gift of all! Jesus Christ is the answer to the question that everyone in this world is asking. I have found that people all over the world struggle with what the meaning of life is all about. If you were asked what life is all about on this Christmas Day, what would you say?

Solomon, the wisest man to ever live, wrote, "Fear God and keep his commandments, for this is the whole duty of man" (Ecclesiastes 12:13b). To "fear God," is to revere Him. It is to live your life in an attitude of worship. In the Bible's story of the first Christmas, we see angels and shepherds, and Mary and Joseph, and wise men and priests all worshipping God. We see men and women submitting themselves to God's plan for their lives. All Advent season we have looked at what it means to be people who seek to honor God by making more disciples for Jesus Christ in the relationships around us, and by growing deeper in our own walks with Jesus. As we end this Advent season, I want to encourage you to look for opportunities to share the love of Jesus even with people you don't know yet. Look for the divine appointments that God brings into your life every day.

Today, there are people who have no one to celebrate Christmas with. As you celebrate today, pray for those who are all alone. Pray for those who have no hope. Pray for those who need a friend. Pray for those who have been shunned by everyone around them. Pray for those who are genuinely seeking God and don't know how to find Him.

Jeremiah 29:13 promises us that, "You will seek me and find me, when you seek me with all your heart."

A popular bumper sticker around the Christmas season says, "Wise men still seek Him." What if God wanted to use you to reach a stranger for Him? What If God wanted to use you to reach a spiritual seeker?

Not long after Jesus ascended into heaven, a man named Philip was given an incredible opportunity to share about Jesus with a man he had never met. In Acts 8:26, an angel of the Lord appeared to Philip and told him to go to a certain place. When Philip arrived he saw a man, who was reading a scroll of Isaiah. The man didn't understand what he was reading. Just then, the Spirit of the Lord told Philip to join him in his chariot.

"So Philip ran to him and heard him reading Isaiah the prophet and asked, 'Do you understand what you are reading?' And he said, 'How can I, unless someone guides me?' And he invited Philip to come up and sit with him" (Acts 8:30-31).

By the end of the story, the man places His faith in Jesus Christ.

I notice a few things about Philip in this story.

- **He was obedient to the voice of God in His life.** When God told Him to get up and go to a certain place, he went. I'm sure that many of us would struggle with such a command. The angel didn't tell Philip why he wanted him to go to the desert, he just told him to go. Are you willing to obey God even when He doesn't give you the full story as to why?
- **He wanted other people to know about Jesus.** When the Spirit instructed Him to join the man in the chariot, Philip went. Why? Because, not only was he obedient, he had a heart for others. This stranger needed something that Philip had. He needed Jesus! So does everyone you know that hasn't placed their faith in Christ.
- **He trusted God to guide him in what to say.** God led Philip to talk to a man from a different part of the world. Philip's culture was completely different than that of the Ethiopian man. But it didn't matter. Philip knew that God would guide him in what to say.

Jesus has commanded all His followers to join Him in His mission of making more disciples. This Christmas, offer Jesus the gift of obedience. Join Him on His mission. Ask Him if even on this Christmas Day there might be a divine appointment for you. It might be that the divine appointment is going to happen in your own home today. God is going to do some great things around the world today. May you and your family be a part of His great adventure!

FAMILY DISCUSSION

- Can you think of a time that God has blessed you with the chance to represent Him to someone that you didn't know?
- God does great things every day. How can we be more purposeful as a family in seeking to be a part of God's story?
- Read the Christmas Story from Luke 2:1-20.

READ

The Christmas Story

Luke 2:1-20

1 In those days a decree went out from Caesar Augustus that all the world should be registered. 2 This was the first registration when Quirinius was governor of Syria. 3 And all went to be registered, each to his own town. 4 And Joseph also went up from Galilee, from the town of Nazareth, to Judea, to the city of David, which is called Bethlehem, because he was of the house and lineage of David, 5 to be registered with Mary, his betrothed, who was with child. 6 And while they were there, the time came for her to give birth. 7 And she gave birth to her firstborn son and wrapped him in swaddling cloths and laid him in a manger, because there was no place for them in the inn.

8 And in the same region there were shepherds out in the field, keeping watch over their flock by night. 9 And an angel of the Lord appeared to them, and the glory of the Lord shone around them, and they were filled with great fear. 10 And the angel said to them, "Fear not, for behold, I bring you good news of great joy that will be for all the people. 11 For unto you is born this day in the city of David a Savior, who is Christ the Lord. 12 And this will be a sign for you: you will find a baby wrapped in swaddling cloths and lying in a manger." 13 And suddenly there was with the angel a multitude of the heavenly host praising God and saying,

14 "Glory to God in the highest,

  and on earth peace among those with whom he is pleased!"

15 When the angels went away from them into heaven, the shepherds said to one another, "Let us go over to Bethlehem and see this thing that has happened, which the Lord has made known to us." 16 And they went with haste and found Mary and Joseph, and the baby lying in a manger. 17 And when they saw it, they made known the saying that had been told them concerning this child. 18 And all who heard it wondered at what the shepherds told them. 19 But Mary treasured up all these things, pondering them in her heart. 20 And the shepherds returned, glorifying and praising God for all they had heard and seen, as it had been told them.

PRAYER

Dear Heavenly Father,

Thank you for the past 30 days that we have had to prepare our hearts and minds for Christmas. Help us take the lessons that we have learned over these 30 days and use them to glorify you. Thank you for the gift of Jesus. May we live our lives for your glory and in obedience to you.

In Jesus' name, Amen.

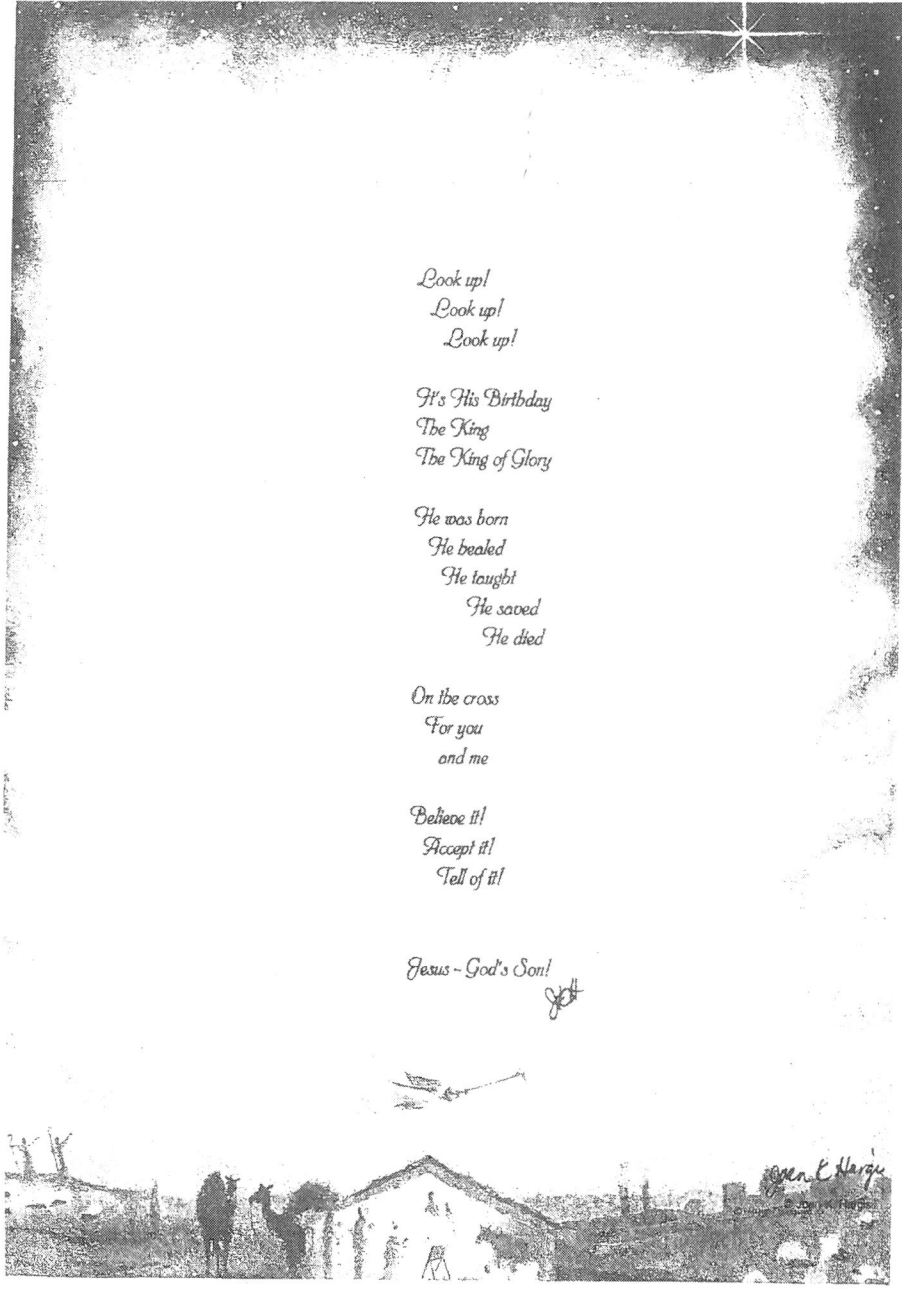

Look up!
 Look up!
  Look up!

It's His Birthday
 The King
  The King of Glory

He was born
 He healed
  He taught
   He saved
    He died

On the cross
 For you
  and me

Believe it!
 Accept it!
  Tell of it!

Jesus ~ God's Son!

Made in the USA
Lexington, KY
18 November 2016